Praise for "Southern

"Southern Fried Rice tells the overlooked hist[...] the Deep South through the author's accoun[...] in Georgia running a laundry from the late 1920s through the 1950s. This inside view of an immigrant family who struggled to make a living and to maintain connections with their Chinese heritage and homeland highlights the mutability and complexity of Chinese American identity and the frequently forgotten ethnic and racial diversity of the South."

Krystyn Moon, Assistant Professor of History, Mary Washington University, Author, Yellowface: Creating the Chinese in American Popular Music and Performance, 1850s-1920s.

"A humane and personal reflection on life as a young Chinese American growing up in Macon, Georgia, when Jim Crow segregation still ruled. This memoir has an incisive clarity that shines extra light on the mundane oddities and inhuman logic of everyday life in the South before the Civil Rights era. It provides a sense of what it was to be like to grow up an outsider in a rigid racial system that could not find a place for those who contradicted its premises and offers us a rare glimpse at the fairly common experience of those who found themselves in the impossible spaces of the American racial order, a world that is both thankfully distant and yet hauntingly familiar still."

Henry Yu, Associate Professor of History, UCLA and University of British Columbia, Author, Thinking Orientals: Migration, Contact, and Exoticism in Modern America

"Southern Fried Rice demonstrates the fluidity of regional and national identity and is both a construction and deconstruction of "Chinese-ness."...These stories offer much toward confirming and complicating popular notions of what it means to be "American" just as it traces the slippery identity shifts of what it means to be "Chinese" ... a valuable mirror that will help move the history of those who are neither Black nor White towards a more deserving central role in the national and international human story."

Stephanie Y. Evans, Assistant Professor of African American Studies and Women's Studies, University of Florida, Author, "Black Women in the Ivory Tower, 1850-1954: An Intellectual History"

"John Jung provides an insightful account of himself and his family in the context of Chinese immigrants who lived in the American South during the 1940s and 1950s. The unique experiences and struggles of his family members serve both to confirm some principles from social science research on Chinese in America as well as to remind us of the importance of individual differences, yielding meaningfulness and substance to issues of culture, race relations, immigration, and identity development. This engaging, candid, and often humorous and heartwarming book is an important contribution not only to the fields of psychology, sociology, and history but also to literature. Social scientists and students alike will find the book immensely fascinating and satisfying."

Stanley Sue. Distinguished Professor, Psychology and Asian American Studies, University of California, Davis   Editor, "Asian American Mental Health: Assessment Theories Methods"

"A charming and engrossing self-ethnography. More importantly, John Jung's book enhances the archive on Asians in the South as well as our understanding of how Jim Crow situated the Chinese between 'white' and 'colored.'"

Leslie Bow, English and Asian American Studies (Director) University of Wisconsin Author "Betrayal and Other Acts of Subversion: Feminism, Sexual Politics, Asian American Women's Literature"

"In Southern Fried Rice, John Jung offers an intriguing and unique perspective on American immigration. Based on his experience as a child in the only Chinese family in Macon, Georgia in the mid-20th century, Jung's story is a fascinating account of the negotiation of personal and ethnic identity in a foreign environment. His narrative highlights many of the features of the larger society, including both government policy and situational practice, that shape the lives of immigrants, both then and now."

Kay Deaux, Distinguished Professor, Psychology, City University of New York Graduate Center, Author, "To Be An Immigrant"

Southern Fried Rice

Life In A Chinese Laundry

In The Deep South

John Jung

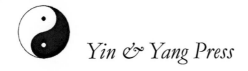 *Yin & Yang Press*

LCCN: 2005-905657
ISBN: 1466218924; 9781466218925

Jung, John 1937-

Southern Fried Rice: Life in A Chinese Laundry in the Deep South

/ John Jung

p. cm.

Includes bibliographical references.

1. Chinese Americans -- Georgia -- Macon -- Biography.
2. Chinese Americans -- California -- San Francisco -- Biography.
3. Laundry workers -- Georgia -- Macon -- Biography.
4. Laundry workers -- California -- San Francisco -- Biography.
5. Immigrants -- Georgia -- Macon -- Biography.
6. Jung, John, 1937- -- Childhood and youth.
7. Jung, John, 1937- --8. Family. Jung family.
I. Title

F294.M2 2005   dc21   975.8/042092; B

Front Cover Design by Lauren Doege

Third Printing, 2011

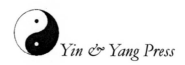

Yin & Yang Press

Dedicated to

Chinese immigrant women
Of the Deep South,
Enduring years of cultural
Isolation, racism, and poverty,
Raising their children to
Overcome all obstacles

Foreword

John Jung's delightful book opens a window providing a glimpse into the lives of one family born to Chinese immigrant parents in a small town in the South in the 1930s and 1940s. Being the only Chinese in town in a segregated society, their lives were certainly not mint julep and magnolias. *Southern Fried Rice* describes the process of running a laundry and the difficulty of raising children isolated from other Chinese before the family moved to San Francisco to live within a Chinese community. Through it all, the family, itself, remained steadfast in their cultural traits and folkways. The author sees his upbringing, and that of his siblings, as the challenging task of accommodating two worlds and, being more Chinese than not.

Quan Shee, or Grace, the author's mother, was truly a woman warrior. She raised her children, worked in the family business and, perhaps, later came to understand the world of finance far better than her husband, and all the while pulling on her own creativity and resources. It may have been many years that she was a lone Chinese woman in town but she never deterred from her vision for the betterment of her family and herself. Bravo!

Sylvia Sun Minnick
Samfow, The San Joaquin Chinese Experience

Preface

Southern Fried Rice tells a personal story that calls attention to an overlooked aspect of the history of the Chinese in America. Unlike most immigrants from Guangdong villages who lived and worked in communities along the Pacific coast from the late 1800s to the middle of the twentieth century, a handful settled in the Deep South. This account of the experiences of one such family offers a glimpse of what life was like for Chinese immigrant families in the South, unable to enjoy connections and cultural practices with other Chinese, while at the same time, being victimized by the staunch racial prejudice of the region.

What was it like to be entirely isolated culturally? We were the only Chinese in the entire city of Macon, Georgia, where we lived above our laundry between 1928 and 1952. During those years racial segregation and Jim Crow were firmly entrenched and entirely legal in the Deep South. My three siblings and I, all born in Macon, were always acutely aware of racial discrimination, and expected to experience it ourselves because, as our parents carefully taught us, we were Chinese but everyone else was either black or white. We were occasional objects of ridicule and curiosity, taunted rather than threatened. These reactions from the community, combined with our ethnic isolation, often made us children ambivalent about being Chinese.

In due time, the lack of contact with a Chinese community forced our parents, and other immigrants with children approaching adulthood, to face the difficult choice between staying in the South or moving to places that had a Chinese community. My parents chose to move across the whole country to San Francisco because they wished us to meet other Chinese people, acquire Chinese values, learn Chinese traditions, and eventually marry other Chinese.

What was it like for a Chinese family, long accustomed to living without contact with its culture, to move to a community with a large Chinese population? Our nearly overnight shift from cultural isolation to cultural immersion held many new challenges. Now living in the midst of the Chinese community in San Francisco, we children were curious and eager to learn about Chinese culture and its traditions. Of course, we children wanted to be accepted by other Chinese but this was not easy for we first had to learn a different way of "being Chinese."

We did not escape racial divisions by moving to San Francisco. As in the South, white prejudices treated Chinese as inferior. Oddly, we may have faced *less* discrimination in Macon, because being the only Chinese there we were not considered a threat. I also discovered, to my surprise, that Chinese sometimes *chose* to isolate themselves. At first, I assumed that this tendency stemmed from their acceptance of white superiority but at other times it seemed that Chinese believed *they* were the superior ones. This self-imposed segregation was a new and uncomfortable experience about which I had mixed feelings.

For my parents their ability to speak and read Chinese eased their transition, but they too had to adjust, as it had been many years since they had lived in a Chinese community. Essentially reborn, and liberated from their years of loneliness in Macon, they rediscovered and enjoyed familiar Chinese traditions, customs, and ways.

Writing this memoir has given me a deeper understanding of the social and psychological forces that shaped me as a person of Chinese descent living in America. My ethnic identity fluctuated widely depending on whether the region in which I was living included few or many other Chinese. Interestingly, this factor is entirely overlooked by most theories of personality development. I hope that this account of my personal experiences will further the study and understanding of the lives of other second-generation ethnic minorities as they struggle to resolve the inevitable conflicts between American values and those of their immigrant parents.

Growing up Chinese in the South provided me with an understanding of what it means to be Chinese-American that is different from what it means for those raised in areas with many Chinese. Far from being a homogenous group often assumed by outsiders, Chinese Americans vary considerably. These differences will undoubtedly become wider in the future. The greater opportunities afforded from the weakening of discriminatory barriers will allow more individualized experiences for everyone.

Acknowledgments

I am indebted to many who encouraged and advised me on undertaking this personal narrative. Conversations with relatives, some who I either met for the first time or had not had the opportunity speak with in years proved very informative. I am grateful to Henry Jew, William Lau, Homer Cheung, Haven Cheung, Harry Cheung, Dominic Lo, Veronica Chang, Grace Lo, Young Quan, Kim Sheng, June Loo, James Chin, and Helen Chin who helped fill gaps and correct misconceptions. I enjoyed the enthusiastic support and approval of this memoir by my sisters, Mary Gee and Jean Oh. Mary's detailed genealogical research over several years, with the aid of other relatives, detailed our father's side of the family and proved invaluable in helping me understand our family history.

My dear friend and colleague, Professor Xiaolan Bao of the Department of History at California State University, Long Beach, set this project in motion, persuading me that this story held value, especially to historians of Chinese immigrants from Guangdong and nearby regions from the period of about 1850 to 1950. She offered needed inspiration and direction.

Several colleagues and associates read the entire manuscript and helped form its focus and structure. Sylvia Sun Minnick gave generously of her time and wisdom in guiding me on this undertaking with abundant cheerful support and editorial advice.

Professor Emerita Judy Yung of the Department of American Studies at the University of California, Santa Cruz, generously provided prompt valuable guidance, information, and encouragement. Enthusiastic support and helpful suggestions also came from Professor Barbara Kim, of the Department of Asian American Studies at CSU, Long Beach and from a former student, Dr. Christine Iijima Hall of the Maricopa Community Colleges.

I am thankful for the thorough and diligent research assistance in the history of Chinese in Macon around the start of the 20th century from Dr. Christopher Stokes of the Washington Memorial Library, the very place that got me hooked on books many years ago. Suzette Raney and the staff of the Chattanooga public library provided valuable evidence about the history of Chinese laundries in that region.

I am grateful to Jeff Jung, Phyllis Jung, and especially, Margo Fiebert for their diligent and thorough reading of the entire manuscript; their suggestions and editing greatly improved its clarity and readability.

Interested readers can find more background other material about Chinese laundries and their place in Chinese American history at www.jrjung.tripod.com.

JJ

November 2005

Contents

Southern Fried Rice

Life In A Chinese Laundry
In The Deep South

1. Why We Were In the Deep South

Most people, even other Chinese, assume that because I am of Chinese ancestry and live in California I must have been born or at least raised in a region with a large Chinese population such as San Francisco. When they discover that I was born and grew up in the middle of Georgia they are usually surprised and ask, "How did you ever end up down there?"

The simplest answer is that when my parents emigrated from a small village near Canton, now called Guangzhou, in southern China to the United States in the 1920s, the only people they knew who could help them get settled in the U. S. happened to be Chinese from their village who were already living in the South. But that answer only leads to the next question about why those Chinese went to the South. The answer is probably similar to that of how my parents found themselves in Georgia. Ultimately, the inquiry becomes an historical query to determine how the first link in the chain between our family village in China and the American South was forged.

From the middle of the nineteenth and well into the twentieth century most Chinese coming to America disembarked in ports on the Pacific coast such as San Francisco or Seattle. The 1848 Gold Rush in California lured many young Chinese men to America; however, opportunities for Chinese immigrants to mine for gold were restricted by racial prejudice. In the mid 1850s, white labor contractors sought unskilled Chinese laborers to help build the American railroads. Unscrupulous practices were often used to mislead or even kidnap Chinese into a form of indentured servitude known as coolie labor.

After these illegal means were outlawed in the 1885, contractors recruited voluntary laborers using a credit-ticket system[1] that paid for the immigrants' passage to America, which would later be repaid with interest out of their wages.

After the completion of the transcontinental railroad in 1869, few work opportunities were available to Chinese workers although for a few years some found work building smaller railroads throughout the country. With an increasing number of Chinese immigrants arriving just as an economic depression hit the United States in the 1870s, heightened discrimination and racial prejudice against the Chinese became widespread. Chinese laborers had earned a reputation as hard workers, doing dangerous tasks, and accepting lower wages than whites. As a result of the economic competition, they were castigated as the "yellow peril." Strong anti-Chinese sentiment had led to numerous laws restricting them, among which were laws curtailing their economic opportunities and jeopardizing their civil rights. In 1882, the U. S. government passed the Chinese Exclusion Act that further blocked immigration of laborers from China. However, Chinese merchants, and their families were still allowed entry under the 1882 exclusion law to allow U. S. - China trade to continue. This law, the only law ever passed against a single ethnic group, remained in effect until 1943, when more favorable attitudes developed because China became an ally against Japan in World War II. Even then, the

---

[1] Thomas W. Chinn, H. Mark Lai, and Philip P. Choy (editors) *"A History of Chinese in California: A Syllabus,"* (San Francisco, CA.: Chinese Historical Society, 1969)

change was mainly symbolic as only 105 Chinese per year were allowed to enter the country.

Due to the increasingly hostile treatment from whites, who reacted with riots and violence to the threat of cheap Chinese labor, many Chinese fled from cities into rural and farming areas away from the West coast. Others moved to urban areas in the East and Midwest such as Boston, Baltimore, New York, Chicago and St. Louis.

One exception was a colony of Chinese who settled in the Mississippi delta area shortly after the end of the Civil War in 1865.[2] The end of slavery disrupted the labor situation, and many freed slaves were no longer available to work on the plantations under terms set by whites. Because of the reputation the Chinese had earned as hard and reliable workers building railroads, farming, and fishing, a meeting of planters was convened in 1862 in Memphis to decide whether to hire 200 men brought from China into the U. S. through New Orleans to help offset the loss of slave labor in the fields. However, working on plantations proved to not be agreeable to the Mississippi Chinese in delta towns like Greenville, and eventually, many began operating small family-owned businesses such as grocery and general stores in poor neighborhoods, mainly serving the Chinese and black populations.[3]

---

[2] Lucy M. Cohen, *"Chinese in the post-civil war South: A people without a history"* (Baton Rouge, La.: Louisiana State University Press, 1984), John Thornell, "Struggle for identity in the most southern place on earth: The Chinese in the Mississippi Delta," *Chinese America, History and Perspectives, 2003.* (San Francisco: Chinese Historical Society of America) 63-70, Robert S. Quan, *"Lotus among the magnolias: The Mississippi Chinese"* (Jackson, Miss.: University of Mississippi Press. 1982)

[3] James W. Loewen, *"The Mississippi Chinese: Between Black and White"* (Prospect Heights, Ill.: Waveland Press, Second Edition, 1988)

Unlike in other regions across the U.S., Chinese did not run laundries in these rural communities.[4] Caught in the middle between the whites and blacks in a racially segregated society,[5] the Mississippi Chinese functioned as a middle group that could work with both whites and blacks.

Perhaps because of the small town and rural areas in which the delta Chinese lived, they were able to create and maintain a strong community that preserved Chinese culture and traditions for themselves, and for their children. Chinese language classes were provided to the children. Community activities centering on Chinese cultural events fostered a strong ethnic identity among the small pockets of Chinese immigrants living in the delta.

The Chinese in southern states further east arrived under quite different circumstances. In 1873, a handful of Chinese was recruited for work on the expansion of a vital canal in Augusta, Georgia.[6] Several hundred Chinese laborers were recruited from the Indianapolis area where they had probably migrated to after work on the transcontinental railroad was completed at Promontory Point, Utah in 1869. Many of them accepted whatever work they could find in the

---

[4] Interview Nov. 29, 2003 with Carl Hoover Lee, long time resident and former Mayor of Louise, Ms.

[5] Although Chinese were admitted to white schools before blacks were allowed, initially they had to attend black schools. Baptists, eager to convert Chinese to Christianity, offered Chinese the alternative of mission schools. Sieglinde Lim de Sanchez, "Crafting a Delta Chinese Community: Education and Acculturation in Twentieth-Century Southern Baptist Mission Schools," *History of Education Quarterly* 43, no.1 (2003): 74-90.

[6] Sally Ken, "The Chinese Community of Augusta, Georgia from 1873 to 1971," *Richmond County History*, 4 no. 1(1972): 51-60. Thomas Ganschow, "The Chinese in Augusta: A historical sketch," *Richmond County History*, 20 (1987): 8-21.

surrounding areas, often involving subservient roles as domestic servants who cooked, cleaned, and laundered clothes for white households. However, these activities, disdained by whites, served as steppingstones for Chinese toward better future occupations.[7] Others drifted back to the West coast or headed toward the east or south as laborers, farmers, and construction workers.

The Augusta canal required two years to complete, and then these Chinese were without jobs. Some moved on, but others stayed in the region. By starting their own businesses, primarily family-run grocery stores similar to those started by Mississippi delta Chinese, along with a few restaurants, laundries, and stores with Chinese goods, they formed the foundation for a small Chinese community in Augusta. Similarly, a small community of Chinese developed in Chattanooga, Tennessee, with over 20 Chinese laundries operating there from around 1880 to around 1930. An examination of City Directories, however, suggests that the Chinese community in Chattanooga dwindled quickly after 1900. A similar trend occurred in other towns and cities. Thus, in 1910, Atlanta had numerous Chinese laundries with close to 100 Chinese residents, according to U. S. Census records. In Macon, where we were the only Chinese when our parents moved there in 1928, there had been three Chinese laundrymen at the turn of the century and as many as eleven Chinese

---

[7] Terry Abraham, "Stepping stones to empowerment: Chinese servants in the American West," <http://www.uidaho.edu/special-collections/papers/stepping.htm> (5 May 2005)
Terry Abraham. "Class, Gender, and Race: Chinese Servants in the North American West." <http://www.uidaho.edu/special-collections/papers/chservnt.htm> (2 June 2005)

in 1908.[8]

This decline in the number of Chinese during this period was not limited to Southern towns. Those men who came to the U. S. in the late 1800s as young men may have either moved, died, or retired to return to China by the early 1900s. Also, stricter enforcement of immigration laws curtailed Chinese immigration to all parts of the U. S. And, by the middle of the last century, newer immigrants may have seen better opportunities in other parts of the country. In any case, eventually, some of these Chinese left jobs involving manual labor such as construction and farming in search of opportunities to become merchants or entrepreneurs so they could have more control over their work and be less dependent on the whims of employers.

The Chinese Hand Laundry

CHINESE LAUNDRY[9]

The Chinese family screened by a wall of steam
Soaks its pride in white bleach
Scrubs the ring around the collar of racial slurs
Rinses with its tears of humiliation
Presses with the starch of its courage

Washing dirty laundry was one job that whites did not care to

---

[8] The Macon City Directory showed that the laundry we operated was in the same location on Mulberry Street as early as 1888. The U. S. Census listed three Chinese residing in Macon in 1910 and showed four Chinese working as laundrymen in 1920. A local newspaper article describing the customs associated with the upcoming celebration of Chinese New Year reported there were 'some eleven members,' or 'celestials' as they were called in that era, in the 'Chinese colony of Macon', *Macon Daily Telegraph*, January 26, 1908, 4A. But by the early 1930s, we were the only Chinese left in Macon.

[9] In memory of Gee Chun, one of the earliest Chinese laundry operators in Edmonton, Alberta, Canada (1895) © Jocelyne Verret from *People From Here And Afar* Collection Littart, Edmonton, Alberta, Canada. By permission of author.

do, so they were willing to cede this occupation to the Chinese.

Moreover, the Chinese did not need much training to operate laundries. Their experience gained from other types of jobs with rigorous physical challenges such as mining, farming, fishing, and railroad construction may have helped the Chinese to withstand the physical demands of running hand laundries.

From about the 1870s until well into the twentieth century, the Chinese laundry was the major occupation of Chinese immigrants and they dominated the laundry business in many communities. These Chinese had not been laundrymen in their country but fell into this work to survive in America. Operating a laundry required relatively little capital,[10]education, or English speaking ability, and it was something that whites did not, at least initially, try to prevent them from doing.[11] It was the primary occupation for Chinese after the major demand for railroad construction work ended after 1869 until around 1900, with other Chinese opening small neighborhood grocery stores and restaurants. Chinese hand laundries sprang up all over the

[10] Compared with a business requiring a large inventory of goods, less capital was needed, but even so, the cost was still beyond the means of new immigrants. A newcomer would earn such small wages working in a laundry that it would require many years to be able to afford to buy his own laundry, pay the rent and wages, pay for utilities and supplies, etc. And, given the low income generated by even a successful laundry, it would have probably been necessary for most laundries to be shared with partners and/or involve unpaid labor by all family members to turn a profit. Some lost money and had to close, especially when competition from other laundries, Chinese or non-Chinese, was strong. Anthony B. Chan, *"Gold Mountain: The Chinese in the New World"* (Vancouver, Canada: New Star, 1983)

[11] See Renqiu Yu, *"To Save China, to Save Ourselves: The Chinese Hand Laundry Alliance of New York"* (Philadelphia, PA.: Temple University Press, 1992) for a history of the growth of Chinese laundries and analyses of the predicaments that the laundrymen faced. He also describes the origin of the Chinese Hand Laundry Association formed by independent laundrymen in New York City in 1933 to fight for fair treatment of Chinese in America as well as to raise money to help China fight the invading Japanese during World War II.

U. S. in small as well as in large cities during the first half of the twentieth century, as well as in other parts of the world.[12] Even though individuals owned them, they had an unmistakable look, almost as if they were franchises. Many had store-window signs with the name of the laundry such as "Loo Ling Laundry" in large black block letters. All of them used tickets printed with some Chinese characters on them, and probably purchased from the same printer in Chicago.[13]

Laundries played a central role for generations of Chinese immigrants, not just in the U. S. but also in other parts of the world. For early Chinese immigrants, the hand laundry provided them one of the few means for self-employment not controlled by whites. Working as servants or farmers did not enable Chinese to save money or be independent whereas operating a laundry allowed the hard working, frugal Chinese to gradually accumulate sufficient funds for their families either here or in China.

White-owned laundries, aided by discriminatory laws,

---

[12] A remarkably similar chain of events led Chinese to start laundry businesses in other countries. In the middle 1800s Chinese were attracted to other places than California where gold was found such as Oregon, western Canada, and New Zealand. Racial prejudices denied them opportunities in gold mining and they ended up in domestic work such as washing and cooking that led them eventually into opening laundries and restaurants. For a history of Chinese laundries in Canada: Ban Seng Hoe, *Enduring hardship: The Chinese laundry in Canada.* (Gatineau, Canada: Canadian Museum of Civilization, 2003) For a history of Chinese laundries in New Zealand, see James Ng, (5/15/03) *A laundry background.* Feb. 28, 2005 <http://www.stevenyoung.co.nz/chinesevoice/history/lanundrymay03.htm> (15 May 2005)

[13] The definitive study of early laundrymen by Paul Siu examined laundries run by one or a few, typically, unmarried Chinese men. Sui described the physical facilities in detail as well as provided a poignant picture of the long and difficult work by these lonely men. Paul C P. Siu, *"The Chinese laundryman: A study of social isolation"* ed. John K. W. Tchen (New York: New York University Press, 1987). Joan S. Wang wrote a doctoral thesis with an excellent analysis of the geographic and economic factors affecting competition with other laundries, both Chinese and white. " 'No tickee, no shirtee:' Chinese laundries in the social context of the eastern United States, 1882-1943" (Ph.D. dissertation, Carnegie-Mellon University, 1996)

competed aggressively with the Chinese. In the 1880s San Francisco passed laws to ban laundries in wood buildings because they represented fire hazards. Other laws forbade laundry operators to work after a certain hour or from living on the premises. These laws were designed against the Chinese for they just happened in live in their laundries, which were located in wood buildings. But the Chinese fought and overcame these legal obstacles. In 1886, they got a favorable ruling by the U. S. Supreme Court in the case of Yick Wo v. Hopkins[14] over the law that prohibited laundries in wooden buildings because this law had a much more adverse impact on the Chinese, as it violated the 14th Amendment to the Constitution provision for the Equal Protection of Rights.

In contrast to small Chinese hand laundries, white laundries started in the 1850s were factory-sized power laundries that used steam engines to supply energy for washing and ironing machinery that could handle much larger volumes of laundry.[15] But one competitive advantage held by the Chinese was that clothes washed by hand were much less likely to be damaged than those run through the machines of the steam laundries.[16] Eventually, however, many Chinese converted

---

[14] Yick Wo *v.* Hopkins, 118 U.S. 356 (1886)

[15] Arwen P. Mohun "Steam laundries: Gender, technology, and work in the United States and Great Britain, 1880-1940" (Baltimore: Johns Hopkins University Press, 1999)

[16] As Chinese laundries charged less, they were a threat to the white power laundries that derided them as using primitive methods compared to their technologically superior machines. White laundries also claimed more hygienic conditions, but that tactic backfired as many feared power laundries for that very reason as they combined clothes from many people in their machines. Joan Wang "Gender, race and civilization: The Competition Between American Power Laundries and Chinese Steam Laundries, 1870s-1920s," *American Studies International* 40 (2002): 52-74.

from hand laundering to the use of steam-powered equipment.

In the southeastern United States many of the Chinese laundrymen came from the same rural villages of Guangdong province. Survival was more likely if immigrants initially settled near relatives and friends from the country of origin. Thus, 19 or 20 of the male descendants of my great, great grandfather came to own or operate Chinese laundries[17] in Georgia and its neighboring states of Alabama and Tennessee starting from about 1915 and operating until the 1960s. In fact, one laundry owned by three generations of the same family still operates in Atlanta.

Five of his grandsons, and nine great grandsons, left China to escape economic hardship in the early part of the last century and ended in the Deep South running laundries. This could hardly have happened by chance. More likely, the first of his descendants to leave China headed for the Deep South because he had either a relative or a friend from his village there who helped him get settled. This conjecture does not address the question of why these earlier Chinese got to the region. This pathfinder might well have been in the South as early as the 1870s as one of the workers recruited from China to help

---

[17] The stereotype of Chinese immigrants as laundrymen applied to my male kin in the South. Somehow, the earliest one to venture here began doing laundry to survive because no other form of work was available, either due to racial prejudice, lack of English language skills, or both factors. Running laundries was a blessing in disguise. Unlike manual labor jobs that are subject to the vagaries of demand and the whims of employers, the laundry owner was his own boss. Chinese laundrymen were able to survive, and save enough to send funds back to their poor families in China. They also supported their children through their college education. Without the laundry as an economic engine, it is unlikely that my kinsmen's children, and grandchildren, would have been as successful as they have been. Their offspring have so far included an architect, engineers, professors, dentists, pharmacists, doctors, accountants, systems analysts, an oncologist, an art therapist, and a biophysicist. For the Chinese, gold was not in the hills of California but in the dirty clothes of its residents.

build the canals in Augusta or perhaps someone who worked on the building of the Alabama and Chattanooga Railroad, a venture that failed leaving almost 1,000 Chinese workers needing other means of survival.[18]

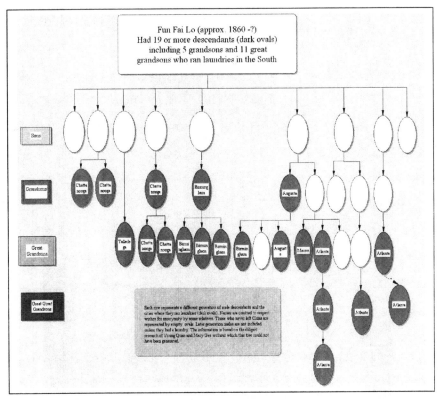

Figure 1   Chinese Laundries (shaded ovals) run by my Father's kin in the South

When these construction jobs ended, he may have stayed in the area and turned to operating a laundry, one of the few work opportunities available to Chinese. Once he gained a toehold financially by owning his own business rather than working for wages,

---

[18] Actually most of these laborers were moved to Louisiana plantations. Cohen, 1984: 82-104.

he probably encouraged other male relatives to come. These later ones would have probably stayed temporarily with one of the earlier arriving kinsmen to apprentice and to save money so they could open their own laundry. They may have opened laundries in nearby towns or acquired laundries from elderly Chinese laundrymen who retired to return to China. From these laundries, these men managed to eke out a hard-earned living. In many cases, they raised families in America, and sent money back to help relatives in their villages in Guangdong. There was a favorable exchange rate for American dollars so that the monies remitted from the laundrymen were worth considerably more in China.

Figure 2   Remains in 2004 of family home in Hoi Ping built with Father's aid.

Chinese laundrymen in America did not exactly live in luxury, washing laundry not being an occupation that promised much wealth. The laundrymen had little to spend, and they often lived in back of their shops, cooked their own meals, and had few material luxuries. Many had left their wives and children behind in China thinking that they would eventually return home with newfound wealth, or at least send money to them until they could return. It is somewhat ironic that Chinese immigrants who led frugal existences still managed to send enough money to their relatives in small Guangdong villages to enable some of them to build rather impressive looking family residences.[19]

However, societal change is inevitable even in the ways people clean their clothing. By the 1950s, Chinese laundries, like the drive-in movie theaters that once flourished along major highways, dwindled in number to the point of extinction. This loss was partly because of the wide availability of automatic washing machines for self-service laundromats and for the home along with new, easier to clean fabrics with features such as permanent press. However, the demise of Chinese laundries should not lead us to overlook the vital role they served in the history of Chinese in America.

[19.]These vernacular homes had an inner courtyard to provide light and ventilation. Extended family members occupied rooms that led to the courtyard based on their place in the family hierarchy. Other houses in a village had similar design, and were arranged with narrow passages between houses to protect against bandits. Ronald G. Knapp, "China's traditional rural architecture: a cultural geography of the common house" (Honolulu, HA.: University of Hawaii Press, 1986).

2. How My Parents Entered America

Kwok Fui, my father, was born on May 13, 1901, in Zantsung, a village in Hoi Ping District. This region is near Guangzhou, formerly called Canton, the largest city in Guangdong Province in southeastern China off the South China Sea. He surely knew of the opportunities America offered because earlier immigrants who visited or came back to retire in their villages told of the promise of financial opportunities in the United States. Faced with economic hard times in southern China at the time, like many other young men, he had little choice but to leave his village to seek a livelihood that would also provide income to help his family. In the past, his family had seen more prosperous years when his grandfather had owned land and produced rice wine, but his own father had not been a skillful merchant, and now the family income was meager. As the oldest of three sons, it was Kwok Fui's lot to emigrate to Gam Saan in 1921 to seek his livelihood working in laundries, and send money[20] back to help his parents and relatives in his impoverished village in China. A decade later, he tried to help his two younger brothers come to America, but only one would succeed in gaining entry.

Kwok Fui was rather tall for a Chinese man in those days, almost 6 feet tall, towering over most other Chinese. From a

---

[20] As a child, I wondered how Father could be certain that funds sent would be safely delivered. Chinese trading firms that exported native foods to Chinese in America also delivered mail and financial remittances by courier to families in Guangdong villages. These 'gold mountain firms' known as *jinshanzhuang* established reliable and trusted networks for such transfers. Madeleine Y. Hsu, *"Dreaming of gold, dreaming of home: Transnationalism and migration between the United States and South China, 1882-1943."* (Stanford, CA.: Stanford University Press, 2000): 35-40.

photograph of him as a young man of 20 on his immigration document in Figure 3, he appears thin and rather serious looking.

Figure 3   Father's 1921 identity documents.

As noted in the previous chapter, entry into the United States was denied for most Chinese immigrants by the exclusionary law passed in 1882. To circumvent this discriminatory legislation, Chinese devised ways of illegal entry using false identities.[21]   Since this law allowed Chinese with merchant status already in the U. S. to bring their family members from China, the Chinese realized they could exploit this provision.   By claiming the existence of more sons in China than they actually had, they could sell the immigration papers for the nonexistent sons to unrelated young men or "paper sons" who wanted to come seek their fortune on Gam Saan (Gold Mountain), as the Chinese called America. One reason such false claims were possible was because the San Francisco earthquake and fire in 1906 had destroyed the records of immigrants, and with them the information collected earlier about their true family composition in China. These paper son imposters would attempt to enter the U. S. using their fake paper (*gai chee*) documents.

As the immigration officers became increasingly aware of this method of fraudulent entry, they began rigorous interrogation of immigrants to try to detect "paper sons."   Detailed and numerous questions were asked about the physical and social structure of the villages from which the immigrants allegedly came. Equally detailed questioning was directed toward the family supposedly shared by the "paper son." Separate interrogations would be made of the "paper son" seeking entry and of the "father" and other "relatives" attempting to bring him into the country.   Much was at stake for the immigrant. If major inconsistencies existed among the testimonies, immigration officers might decide to deny entry.

---

[21] Erika Lee. *"At America's Gates: Chinese immigration during the exclusion era, 1882-1943"* (Chapel Hill, N. C.: University of North Carolina Press. 2003)

Kwok Fui, my father, was such a "paper son" and like all other such immigrants, carefully coached with answers for the kinds of questions that would likely be asked. His papers identified him as Jung Ben, the son of Jung Lim, a San Francisco merchant. He had to forsake his real family name, Lo, to use the alleged father's surname, Jung.[22]

An immigration officer went to the place of business in San Francisco operated by the merchant who was Kwok Fui's alleged father to verify his financial resources, as indicated in the document below submitted to the Commissioner of Immigration at Angel Island.

In Re: JUNG BEN, Son of Merchant,
ex SS "Nanking," April 28, 1921.

On the 29th ultimo I visited the firm of Chun Chun Gok and Co., located at 930 Stockton St., San Francisco, California. I found there the Manager, Tow Young How, also the alleged father, in this case, JUNG LIM, a salesman with this firm, holding an active interest of $500.

The personnel of the firm consists of five members, three of whom are active. The firm is capitalized at $4,000 and the value of the stock is placed at $3,000, which, I think is a conservative estimate. The kind of business conducted by this firm is Chinese and American groceries. In addition to the main store room there is a loft which is well stocked with the kind of goods carried by the firm. There is also, so the Manager stated to me, about $450 worth of goods stored in the M. J. B. Warehouse. I have no doubt as to the mercantile status of this firm, and none of the prohibitive features were in evidence.

Immigrant Inspector

Figure 4 Examiner memo verifying Kwok Fui's paper father merchant assets.

---

[22] Chinese and American surnames occur in opposite order, being last for Americans and first for Chinese. The surname of my father, Lo, (Loo, Lau are other forms) preceded his first name, Kwok Fui.

At the immigration hearing, his paper father and paper brother had to appear for questioning. Witnesses also came to testify that they knew father and his alleged relatives. Kwok Fui, in his interview, was asked dozens of questions: the physical layout of the village, which direction the main street faced, features of the house in which he lived, how many windows were on each side of the building, how many doors there were, how many stairs led up to the front door as well as questions about relatives living in the home and where they slept. This was a difficult test as he did not actually know these relatives and had never been in their house. His answers had to agree with those given by his "paper father" as well as those of his "paper brother."

An excerpt from the detailed interrogation of Kwok Fui when he first came to the U. S. in 1921 is presented below. It is typical of the line of questioning employed at these proceedings, not unlike that used in a criminal investigation.

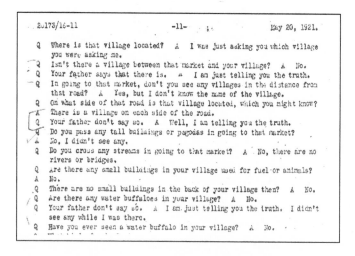

Figure 5 Excerpt from Father's Immigration Interrogation in 1921.

Several times the examiner challenged his answers, indicating that the "paper father" or "paper brother" had responded differently, and asking Kwok Fui why his answers conflicted with theirs. Whether the examiner was 'bluffing' or there were actual discrepancies is unknown but Kwok Fui held his ground and rarely changed his answer, claiming then to have forgotten. He usually asserted that he was telling the truth. His approach was successful, and he was admitted to the U. S.

Those who did manage to successfully enter were then challenged to survive in a land where many of them knew not a word of the language, and none of the customs. They were often victims of racial prejudice and in danger of bodily harm along with mental harassment. Separated from their friends and family, they faced an often hostile reception from whites. Most of the Chinese immigrants from Guangdong province in the early 1900s had been poor in their homeland and lacked education, and in many respects their plight was even worse in the United States.

Kwok Fui's survival, like that of many immigrants, depended on the help of earlier immigrants from his own village. In his case, he had real relatives, although some had different paper names, and they were working in the South operating hand laundries. There are at least two conflicting accounts[23] of how Father came to be in the South, but both involve his receiving assistance from a relative from China who had an already established laundry in this region.

---

[23] Different relatives gave different accounts. Unfortunately, when I was a child I did not have enough interest in the details to ask my parents for their version.

One version[24] suggested he was an apprentice to a grand uncle, Lo Gan Lion, in a laundry in Chattanooga, Tennessee. He then moved to Georgia, where he apprenticed in Augusta working with other relatives from his village in their laundries. While he learned how to run a laundry, he saved enough eventually to buy his own laundry in Macon, Georgia, from an elderly Chinese who was retiring to return to China. It is unclear whether the owner was related to him.

The other account[25] held that his uncle, Lo Gan Hong, who settled in Augusta to run a laundry around 1921, brought Father as well as his own son, Heung Sec, to help him. This uncle, with an American name, Roy Loo, was an influential member of the Augusta Chinese community, and in 1925, a founder of the Chinese Consolidated Benevolent Society, a mutual aid organization.

As in the first version of how Father came to America, as soon as he could afford it, he purchased his own laundry in Macon before returning to China in 1927 to find a wife. It is difficult to confirm which of the two accounts is correct, as many older relatives who I contacted were very reluctant to divulge or confirm immigration details for fear of adverse consequences from federal authorities even after over 85 years have passed since Father first entered the United States.

When, as a child, I first learned from my mother about the "paper son" method for illegal entry to the U. S., I never imagined the

---

[24] Interview in August, 2004 with Young Quan who grew up in his father's laundry in Birmingham, Alabama during the 1940s and later owned his own laundry there.

[25] Interview in August, 2004.with Kim Sheng, daughter of Father's cousin Heung Sec who had a laundry in Augusta, Georgia from the 1920s to late 1950s.

Figure 6 The Chinese Consolidated Benevolent Society of Augusta, 1925. Father's uncle, Lo Gan Hong, is to right of center, front row and Father's cousin, Heung Sec, is at left end of the second row. Courtesy, Georgia Archives.

extent to which the practice occurred. I thought that my parents were somehow an aberrant case, and that most Chinese just came over without deception. I was astounded when, as a college student, I learned that a large percentage of the many thousands of Chinese who entered the U. S. between 1882 and 1943 had to resort to this method of illegal entry. There have been estimates that ninety percent of those using false papers succeeded in gaining entry.[26]

This is a surprisingly high rate since immigration officials made strenuous efforts to detect false papers. Suspicious of Chinese translators, they took precautions to make sure they were not conspiring with their fellow Chinese to aid their entry. On the other

---

[26] Judy Yung, *"Unbound voices: A documentary history of Chinese women in San Francisco"* (Berkeley and Los Angeles, CA.: University of California Press, 1999) :11.

hand, enforcement was poorly funded and rules were confusing to inspectors for over 20 years.[27] Immigrants who had money hired lawyers to appeal adverse rulings, a process that worked in favor of the Chinese in the long run since it gave lawyers access to interrogation transcripts. As this information about the nature of typical questions spread through the community, Chinese prepared elaborate 'crib sheets,' rumored to sometimes be smuggled in baked goods, with information that detainees memorized and then destroyed.[28]

Ambiguity of records may have also hampered enforcement. Interpretation of records was difficult for immigration officials who were often confused because the order of Chinese names is the opposite of Western names, with the surname coming first. Moreover, name spellings differed when translated into English.

An Arranged Marriage

By his late twenties, Father had achieved some financial success in acquiring his own laundry to provide a stable income. After working as an apprentice in Chinese laundries in the South for six years, in 1927 he claimed merchant status as Ben Jung on Milledgeville Road in Augusta. This status would allow him to bring a wife from China back to Georgia, but first he had to go back to Guangdong to find one.

---

[27] Laws are only as good as their implementation. See Chapter 3 in Marie Rose Wong, "Sweet cakes, long journey: The Chinatowns of Portland, Oregon" (Seattle, WA.: University of Washington Press, 2004)

[28] Before 1900 the interviews were often brief but became longer as officials learned that many applicants had purchased false papers. Chinese countered by teaching new applicants what questions to expect and coaching them with details of their false identities such as their family trees, village layout, etc. Estelle T. Lau, *"Paper families: Identity, immigration administration and Chinese exclusion"* (Ph.D. dissertation, University of Chicago, 2000)

The Chinese firmly believed in marrying only other Chinese. Besides, in many regions of the South, miscegenation laws existed that prohibited interracial marriages, even if they were not strictly enforced. Moreover, because of the low status of the Chinese in the United States, the only Americans available for marriage with Chinese were either poor and or from other minority groups.

Figure 7 My father, Lo Kwok Fui, when he married in 1928.

On several occasions as a child, I heard Chinese men ridicule and disparage a Chinese laundryman whose marriage to a white woman had ended in divorce. While a few Chinese laundrymen married non-Chinese women, most of them returned to China to seek Chinese wives until that was curtailed during World War II.

In China marriage occurs at a young age to relieve poverty-stricken families from the burden of supporting children for a long time. For centuries, arranged marriages were the custom. The tradition in China of arranged marriages and governed by economic concerns is unpalatable to Americans who believe in romantic unions where the mates freely choose their "one true love."

Typically, a matchmaker would identify a prospective bride and notify the groom's family. The prospective groom had a chance to view the prospective bride without her knowledge. No actual encounter between them would occur; the prospective groom would simply inform the go-between whether she was a satisfactory match. In contrast, the bride-to-be did not have the same opportunity. If the families agreed to the match, the bride was informed of her betrothal.

The matchmaker for Kwok Fui was his own father. He instructed Kwok Fui to go to the village to take a look at Quan Wai Choi while she was shopping in the Chuck Tom market, unaware that she was being observed for a matrimonial purpose.

Born on Oct. 5, 1909, Wai Choi grew up in Tai Ng, a small village in Hoi Ping District, not far from Father's village. Her father, Kwan Sung Kwong,[29] earned his living by selling preserved shrimp in the village market. Wai Choi was the first child, small in statue, barely 5 ft. tall at adulthood. As the eldest, she had the responsibility of taking care of her younger siblings, two brothers and three sisters. Even as a child she must have been independent and self-reliant, judging from stories she would later tell her children about her childhood. When she was old enough to attend school, her parents could not afford to pay tuition and also felt schooling was a waste for a girl. Nonetheless, she would sometimes sneak off and attend school

---

[29] Kwan and Quan are alternative spellings, but I do not know why Mother spelled it differently from her father.

despite these obstacles. Although she never achieved more than a third grade education, she did read and write Chinese.

Wai Choi was always somewhat serious in her outlook on life. Even in the earliest available photograph of her, taken at the time of her wedding, she bore a concerned look on her face.

Figure 8 Mother at the time of her marriage in 1928.

After Kwok Fui went to the market and secretly observed Wai Choi, he agreed to the match, which the Lo and Quan families then finalized. In this manner, Wai Choi, 20 years old and with no say in the matter, was betrothed to a man eight years her senior on whom she had never laid eyes.

Wai Choi's mother, Leung Shee, then informed her that a marriage agreement had been made for her with the parents of a young man from a neighboring village. She learned that this tall young man had been working for several years in laundries in America and that he had recently returned to find a bride to take back. Marriage was not a choice or issue for her to object to or question; her fate, it was beyond her control. If the match showed promise for leading to economic or social benefit for her as well as for her parents, the feeling was that she should consider herself quite fortunate.

However, marriage to this young man meant not only that she was leaving her family and her village but also her country, and moving to a distant foreign land, the United States, of which she knew virtually nothing. Her move might be for many years, although she probably expected to return to China to retire, as did most of the immigrants from China during this period. Yet, what were her alternatives to this sudden upheaval? If this match had not been proposed, she might remain in poverty in her village, a burden to her family. Still, moving to America was not without considerable risk as well.

What must have been her feelings and concerns about moving to a strange far away land? Certainly she was sad leaving her parents, brothers and sisters. In addition, she must have had more anxiety than eagerness about going to this foreign land, as she certainly had heard that Chinese immigrants were treated there as objects of both scorn and curiosity. And of course, she would also have to adjust to living with someone whom she had never met before, who would be her husband for the rest of her life.

In a matter of a few weeks, the wedding was held in the village in March of 1928. Wai Choi's meager belongings were packed up, and with a small escort of family and friends she was conveyed in a sedan chair from her village over the short distance to the village of her husband-to-be. There a wedding banquet was held in the groom's family home with a small number of guests. When the bride and groom exchanged gifts, Wai Choi would no longer be referred to by her maiden name, but as Quan Shee Lo.[30]

A few months later in July, they departed for Hong Kong where they purchased passage on the ship, S. S. President Lincoln that was to carry them across the Pacific Ocean to start their new lives together in the United States. For about 10 days in Hong Kong while they awaited the required documents, Quan Shee worked to memorize the details of her husband's false identity before the arduous, long voyage across the Pacific. They received careful coaching and notes from Chinese who were familiar with the interrogation process. It was crucial that both of them have the same answers to the questions that would probably be asked at the Immigration Station or else they might be denied entry into the United States.

The Angel Island Immigration Detention Station

Upon reaching San Francisco all Chinese were processed for entry at the Immigration Detention and Quarantine Station built in 1910 on Angel Island in the San Francisco bay. It was within easy view of the hills of San Francisco and near Alcatraz Island, which was not yet a federal prison. Until 1940 when it was closed, an estimated 175,000 Chinese immigrants were detained and interrogated at the Angel Island station before they were either allowed entry or deported.

---

[30] Shee is a title that roughly means "Mrs." We were confused because when we had to give our mother's maiden name on legal forms, she told us it was Quan Shee.

Figure 9 Mother's passport photograph.

Detention usually lasted two to three weeks, but many were detained for several months, or longer while awaiting decisions.[31] Living conditions were austere if not outright deplorable. Men and women had separate common open barracks for sleeping quarters that afforded little or no privacy. Guards were posted outside the locked dormitories. For a while, women were even separated from their children, which created much distress. Communal living quarters held over 100 people who would sleep in bunk beds, stacked three high with little space between the rows.[32] The food was tasteless and bland, quite foreign and certainly different from the diet in China. Sometimes

[31] From 1910 until it was closed in 1940, all Chinese immigrants were quarantined at Angel Island. Detailed interrogations were used to detect immigrants entering under false identities purchased from other Chinese. Connie Y. Yu, "Rediscovered Voices: Chinese Immigrants and Angel Island," *Amerasia Journal* 4 no. 2 (1977): 123-139.

[32] Him Mark Lai, Genny Lim, and Judy Yung, "Island: Poetry and History of Chinese immigrants on Angel Island, 1910-1940" (Seattle, Wa: University of Washington Press, 1991)

rice would be provided, but it was not steamed as the Chinese cook it, so it was not appetizing to the immigrants. Fortunately, by the 1920s they began hiring Chinese cooks who commuted from San Francisco to help resolve this problem.

While waiting for her interrogation, Quan Shee's physical exam revealed she had a hookworm[33] infection that had to be treated before she could be admitted. While in agonizing pain, probably a side effect of the drugs used for treating hookworm, and unable to comprehend the reasons for her detention, she underwent the ordeal of the intensive interrogation of the Immigration officers, knowing that even a minor mistake might prevent her entry into the country. Meanwhile, her husband, who was being readmitted rather than entering for the first time, was allowed to enter San Francisco. There he sought the help of a friend from the old country and obtained legal assistance. Alone and afraid, Quan Shee did not know when, if ever, she would be admitted into the country. She passed her interrogation, but was detained another week or two to complete her treatment for hookworm.

Years later, she often related what a trying ordeal it was when she first arrived in America. She bitterly told her children how cruel it was to be confined like a "jail prisoner" on Angel Island.[34] She cited

---

[33] Hookworm and other parasites were not uncommon among Chinese immigrants, but it was a political issue and not just a health concern. Nayan Shah, *"Contagious divides: Epidemics and race in San Francisco's Chinatown."* ((Berkeley and Los Angeles, CA.: University of California Press, 2001): 189-201.

[34] Many other Chinese at the Angel Island Immigration Detention Center expressed similar sentiments. When it was closed in 1940, a park ranger discovered Chinese characters etched on some of the walls, poems expressing the frustration, anguish, and suffering of detainees.

her experiences as evidence of how much injustice and discrimination Chinese immigrants suffered from the authorities.

Kwok Fui's Second Immigration Interview

Examiners also posed challenges to some answers when Kwok Fui was interrogated in 1928 when he returned to the United States with Quan Shee after their marriage. At one point near the middle of this transcript page, the examiner pointed out a curious aspect of his answers about the structures in his village. Both in 1921 and again in 1928, when asked this question, he had first given one answer and then corrected himself. The examiner confronted him and accused him of lying or giving memorized answers. Kwok Fui must surely have been startled, but he gave no reply other than to insist that he was stating the facts. Unexpectedly, the examiner then backed off, and ended the session. Perhaps, standing firm, instead of changing his answers when challenged made him appear more credible.

```
Q  How many houses were there in the JEW VILLAGE while you were there last?A 12.
Q  When was the last house built in the JEW VILLAGE? A I do not know because at the
time of my birth there were 12 houses.
Q  Why has JEW VILLAGE remained to stationary in its growth?A I do not know why.
Q  While you were in the JEW VILLAGE last was anybody married there?  A No.
Q  While you were in the JEW VILLAGE last did anybody die there?A No.
Q  While you were in the JEW VILLAGE last was anybody born there?A I never heard of
any.
Q  Which way does JEW VILLAGE face and which direction is the head?A It faces south
the head is east.
Q  Counting from the east where is your father's house located? A 4th house, 2nd row
Q  Are the houses in that row all dwelling houses?A Yes.
Q  Have they always been dwelling houses?A No the first house is a lantern house.
Q  How did you happen to make the mistake of saying they were all dwellings?A I
misunderstood.
Q  You were asked that same question when you were an applicant for admission and
you have answered it precisely in the same way you do now.  You first stated that
they were all dwellings and then you changed as you did now.  Are you memorizing
a story or are you stating facts?A I am telling you facts.
```

Figure 10 Excerpt from Kwok Fui's 1928 interview when he returned with Quan Shee.

Him Mark Lai, Genny Lim, and Judy Yung, "*Island: Poetry and History of Chinese Immigrants on Angel Island, 1910-1940*" (Seattle, WA, University of Washington Press, 1991)

Quan Shee's Immigration Interview

Quan Shee faced an equally long and detailed interrogation, involving well over a hundred questions, many of which were very detailed and seemingly arbitrary. Interrogation of women was often directed on ensuring that they were indeed the wives of their alleged husbands. There was suspicion that they might be prostitutes as there were very few Chinese women in America, and some women were in fact being brought in for prostitution.

Two excerpts from the 1928 proceedings reproduced in Figure 11 show that her questions focused on details of the wedding ceremony, who attended, what foods were served, who sat at which table, what the bride wore. Questions about the wedding were not difficult since they had obviously been present but two people can still differ in recall of details. Many of the questions seemed directed at harassing rather than determining if the bride was who she claimed to be. In addition, questions about the villages from which the bride and groom came from such as the physical layout, types and number of houses were included. Quan Shee had never been to Father's village so questions about the physical features of Kwok Fui's village (actually the village of his "paper father") were very difficult. Coached by Kwok Fui, she had to memorize details given to her about the village, her alleged father-in-law, and his family. Answers to these questions from the bride, groom, and witness had to generally agree to convince the examiners. This situation was by no means unique for my parents; it was the case for thousands of "paper sons" who came to America during the Chinese exclusion that extended from 1882 until 1943.

Q How many marriage feasts occurred at the time of your marriage?A One only.
Q When did that take place?A On the 18th day.
Q How many tables were spread for that feast and where were they spread?A Four in our home.
Q At what time of the day did you arrive?A About 4 o'clock in the afternoon.
Q What happened after your arrival? A I was carried into my husband's room.
Q How long did you remain there? A Until the next day.
Q Did you have no part whatever in the marriage ceremony?A I did not take part in any ceremony.
Q How long after your arrival was it that you saw your husband?A It was very late that night.
Q What did you do when you first saw him?A I gave him a cup of tea.
Q Was the tea gold or warm?A I do not know I did not touch the tea.
Q Did you prepare the tea or did someone else prepare it for you?A Somebody else did.
Q Did you serve your husband any wine when you first saw him? A No. (changes) Yes, I gave him two cups.
Q At what time on the following day did you see CHONG YIT SANG? A In the morning I do not know about what hour.
Q Where did you see him? In the parlor of our home.
Q Did you talk to CHONG YIT SANG at that time?A No.
Q Did you not even address greetings to each other?A Yes, I addressed him.

27144/5-15   9-18-28.   Page.19

Q How long did you and he remain in each other's presence?A I just addressed him and then went back to my room, I do not know how long he stayed.
Q On the day after your marriage what persons did you find living in your house? A There were 9 altogether. My father-in-law JUNG LIM, my mother-in-law GIN SHEE, my husband's sister-in-law, I don't know her name, my husband's sister HO HEUNG, my husband's brother JUNG TOON, the son of my husband's brother JUNG SHEUCK whose name is JUNG FOOK SIM, my husband and I.
LEE PARK LIN
~~translation~~/INTERPRETER.
Q Have you understood the previous interpreter?A Yes.

Q You have stated there were 9 persons living in your husband's house on the morning after your marriage and you have named but eight. Who was the 9th person? A I was going to name JUNG SHEUCK among those who were living at the house but he was in the U.S. at that time.
Q How many houses are owned by your husband's family in JEW VILLAGE? A One.
Q Is that house a regular five room dwelling?A Yes.
Q Following your marriage which bedroom in that house did you occupy?A The bedroom on the west side.
Q Did you and your husband occupy that room by yourselves?A Yes.
Q What room was occupied by your husband's parents?A In a room partitioned off in the parlor.
Q Of what was the partition made, how high was it and how did it partition the parlor off?A It was a wooden partition, it extends up to the loft and extends across the back portion of the parlor.
Q Where did the wife and son of JUNG SHEUCK sleep?A In the room on the east side.
Q Did anyone sleep in that room with them?A My husband's sister HO HEUNG.
Q Where did JUNG TOON sleep?A In the ancestral hall.
Q Did you see your alleged husband at any time or place before you arrived at his house the first time?A No.
Q How far and what direction is the AI NG VILLAGE from the JEW VILLAGE? A About three lis away I do not know what direction.
Q When you were living at AI NG VILLAGE were you able to see JEW VILLAGE from there?A Yes.
Q What part of JEW VILLAGE was nearest to the AI NG VILLAGE? A The north side.
Q Who accompanied you when you came to your husband's house to be married? A There were two women attendants, there were some men but I don't know how many.
Q How were you conveyed to your husband's house?A In a sedan chair.

Figure 11 Excerpt from Quan Shee's immigration interview in 1928.

Although she managed to pass the exam, an excerpt from page 23 of the transcript of her interrogation on Sept. 15, 1928, showed that the examiner noticed she failed to identify her alleged father-in-law from his photograph. He must have been suspicious, wondering why she failed to recognize him, given that she had spent the four months after the wedding living in his house. Nonetheless, fortunately, for some unknown reason the examiner finally did accept her testimony![35]

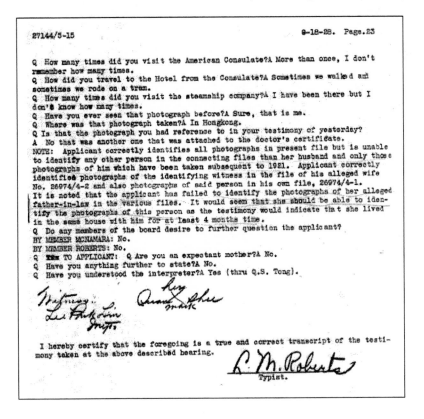

Figure 12   Concluding section of Mother's immigration interview in 1928.

---

[35] It would have been impossible to verify all the facts for any interview. Examiners relied on consistency of answers by asking the same questions repeatedly or by cross checking answers from the applicant and alleged relatives. One view is that they had leeway in deciding who got admitted and who got deported. Lau, 2000.

Then at long last, she was free to enter San Francisco. From there, a few days later, she and Father next had to journey an additional 3,000 miles across the country by train to reach Georgia where she would begin her new life as the wife of a laundryman. At the time she embarked on this journey, little did she realize that she would be venturing into a part of the country that was not very tolerant of foreigners, especially those of a different skin color. Nor did she probably foresee that she and her husband would rarely see other Chinese for many years to come.

3. Living in Macon, Georgia

Most Chinese immigrants preferred to settle in California, if not in San Francisco itself, where there was a community of other Chinese to offer abundant cultural contact and ties to Chinese customs, foods, and rituals. People around them spoke Chinese, providing ample opportunities for socializing as well as sources of assistance and information about how to deal with American customs. And for those unwilling or unable to learn English or adopt American customs, they could survive on a day-to-day basis speaking their native tongue by limiting their interactions to within the Chinese community.

In contrast, scattered throughout small towns in the southern part of the United States were isolated Chinese families. In the case of Quan Shee and Kwok Fui, their family was the only Chinese family in the city of Macon, Georgia, with the nearest other Chinese in Atlanta, 100 miles to the north or in Augusta which was about the same distance but to the northeast near the South Carolina border.[36] Due to their isolation, neither Mother nor Father had other adults around with whom they could speak in Chinese or talk about matters related to their homeland. It was essential to acquire Basic English rapidly, a task that was feasible for Father since he had to deal with English speaking customers. Mother, however, was fully occupied bringing up her children and working in the laundry so her opportunities to learn

---

[36] A sizeable Chinese community in Augusta dates back to the end of the Civil war when Chinese laborers were recruited to replace the freed slaves and to help build the Augusta canal in 1872. By the end of the 19th century, some of these Chinese became grocers and laundrymen. Catherine Brown and Thomas Ganschow, "The Augusta, Georgia, Chinese: 1865-1980," *West Georgia College Studies in the Social Sciences* 22 (1983): 27-41; Thomas Ganschow, "The Chinese in Augusta: A historical sketch," *Richmond County History* 20(1987): 8-21

English were much more limited. In Atlanta and Augusta, around the time my parents moved to Macon there were several Chinese families, as well as bachelors who had never married or had left wives, and in some cases, children in China to seek work in America.[37] In cities with a Chinese community, some sense of cultural contact could be fostered and enjoyed whereas this vital resource was absent for my parents in Macon.

Macon: The Heart of Georgia

Located close to the geographical center of Georgia, Macon had a population of about 50,000 when Mother and Father arrived in 1928. It was not a tiny village, but a small town that prospered as a rail center with a thriving economy based on cotton, textiles, and agriculture. The Ocmulgee River, with its ugly muddy brown waters, ran along the eastern edge of the downtown section. Several blocks west was Mulberry Street, a major street which was the business route for U. S. Highway 41 that linked Florida at least as far north as Chicago. Our laundry, and living quarters above it in what had probably been storage rather than living space, was situated in the middle of town on this wide street with its median tree-lined parks.

Macon was a pleasant enough city, but race relations [38] were not

---

[37] The Immigration Act of 1965 greatly increased the number of Chinese, as well as other Asian immigrants, but the claim of about 30,000 Chinese in Atlanta by the late 1990s by Zhao seems excessive. Jianli Zhao, *"Strangers in the City: The Atlanta Chinese, their community, and stories of their lives."* (New York: Routledge, 2002)

[38] Racial segregation and discrimination has a long history in the South. For a southern city, Macon had a history of moderation on race issues which helped it succeed in dealing with the growing racial tension during the mid to late 1950s. Even when protest marches and sit-ins occurred in the early 1960s, Macon's efforts to desegregate public facilities were commended

as harmonious as they sometimes appeared on the surface. Racial segregation prevailed in Macon, as throughout the South. In education, whites and "colored people"[39] had separate, but decidedly *not* equal school facilities. Although boys and girls went to elementary school together, at the junior high and senior high school level, students were not only separated by race but also by sex. White boys attended Lanier Junior and Senior High Schools and white girls attended Miller Junior and Senior High Schools. At the college level, Macon had two small institutions, Mercer University, a Baptist-affiliated institution for white men and Wesleyan, a Methodist-based college for white women.

Macon's downtown shopping area was small enough to easily cover on foot. The city was physically attractive and generally safe from street crime. It held no outstanding tourist attractions and was not a vacation destination for tourists, leaving it a tranquil and

---

by national media such as the Wall Street Journal. However, by no means was full equality of rights achieved. Racial conflicts and tensions worsened during the 1970s as white backlash developed in the face of the ever increasing demands made by African Americans for their civil rights. Andrew M. Manis, *"Macon Black and White: An unutterable silence in the American century"* (Macon, Ga.: Mercer University Press and Tubman African American Museum, 2004)

[39] *"I was "colored" until I was 14, a Negro until I was 21
And a black man ever since"* Reggie Jackson

"My grandfather was colored, my father was Negro, and I am black."
   Henry Louis Gates, Jr. From his Personal Statement in his admission application to Yale University

Labels for different races are highly charged emotionally. They also change over time, making it difficult to choose terms that are always acceptable or accurate. The label 'black', used as far back as 1400 to refer to peoples of African descent, was unacceptable in the 1800s while 'colored' was favored until it was displaced by 'Negro' in the early 20th century. But the civil rights activism of the 1960s led to the preference of 'black' and 'African American' over 'Negro.' Now in the 21st century, the once rejected label 'black' has resurfaced and gained popular usage. *"The American Heritage Book of English Usage, A Practical and Authoritative Guide to Contemporary English"* (Boston: Houghton Mifflin, 1996). In this memoir 'black' will be used most often but the labels that were used when I was growing up in Macon in the 1940s, 'colored' and 'Negro,' will be used when needed to reflect those times.

somewhat sedate town.

When I was growing up there, it was large enough to support several radio stations, a morning and an evening newspaper, and six movie theaters, five for whites and one for blacks. Television was just arriving and most people did not yet own a set. The nearest television station in 1950 was in Atlanta, about one hundred miles away, with very poor reception in Macon.[40]

Summers were cruelly hot and humid in Macon. Father had some electric fans to circulate the air in the laundry, but the air was still very warm. The heat generated from the ironing and steam pressing of laundry intensified the discomfort. Hell itself could not be much hotter than a Chinese laundry in Georgia during August! At night, during the summer we used oscillating electric fans to circulate the air so we could fall asleep. When the fan would rotate away from your face, you would hold your breath waiting for it to reverse its direction and again send a breeze your way.

During the summer, storms often passed through quickly. The skies would suddenly darken, and there would be the rumble of thunder. Then the rain would pour down heavily, and often lightning would strike accompanied by ear-piercing thunder. Then, just as quickly, the sun would reappear and the humid air would hang like a weight dragging your energy down and down. But lightning that struck at night was really thrilling, because it would light up the whole sky.

---

[40]I went to the Sears Roebuck store to watch a telecast of a baseball game beamed from Atlanta around 1950. It was the first time I had ever seen any television broadcast but it was a major league disappointment for the game looked as if it were being played in a snowstorm.

And, if the lightning came in bolts, it was awe inspiring to behold. However, when I was older and learned that lightning strikes can kill and are unpredictable, I had a new respect and fear of it.

Winter was also unpleasant, although not as much as it would have been in a northern part of the U. S. It was not cold enough in Macon for snow, other than for a few flurries, perhaps once every decade or so. But, it sometimes was below freezing at night, and given that we had no central heating in our spartan living quarters, we had to rely on a small gas burning heater in one room. For safety reasons, it was not left on while we slept, so it was very unpleasant getting out of bed on cold mornings. Downstairs in the laundry, it would be considerably warmer as the day went on because of the heat generated from the operation of the laundry equipment.

My parents settled in a place quite different from the villages they left behind. Moreover, the timing of their arrival in America probably could not have been worse as the Great Depression of the 1930s was about to unfold. Times were difficult for everyone, and Mother had to work from dawn to bedtime everyday except Sunday, often with little nourishing food to eat. She attributed a miscarriage of her first pregnancy to these difficult conditions. She later would relate that Father was neglectful of her physical condition. It was only because some Chinese relative visiting them had reprimanded him that her needs for adequate food were fulfilled.

With the birth of their first child, Mary, in 1931, and then another daughter, Eugenia (Jean) in 1934, Mother had the burden of working in the laundry as well as the tasks of childrearing. At the crack of dawn, she awakened and dressed the young girls each weekday morning. They were reluctant to leave the living quarters on Mulberry Street and go out into the still dark morning, which in winter was rather chilly. She had to coax them along for several blocks to a storefront on Cotton Avenue with the imposing but exaggerated name, Great Southern Laundry that served as a drop off and pick up station for customers. Each evening she would reverse the process and return to the Mulberry Street location where the laundry was actually washed and ironed by Father and his workers, all black women.

Figure 13   Jean and Mary looking after me at the city auditorium.

Eventually they closed the Cotton Ave. satellite laundry office, perhaps as our family increased in size when I was born, increasing the difficulty for Mother to split her time between two sites. The Sam Lee Hand Laundry on Mulberry Street then became our only store.

Despite this demanding and tedious routine, Mother did learn to adopt Western styles of clothing and sometimes dressed nicely on Sundays, the one day of the week when she could relax a little.

Figure 14 Mother dressed in her Sunday best clothes with Mary c. 1936.

During World War II, our laundry was very busy with the added business of soldiers stationed at nearby military bases at Warner Robbins and Camp Wheeler. It was exciting to see the soldiers, neatly dressed in their khaki uniforms with military emblems sewn on their sleeves. We assembled quite a collection of military brass medallions because some soldiers left them in the clothing they brought in to be washed and never claimed them.

Even though the war was thousands of miles away, occasionally, there would be air raid drills at night and we would see searchlights scanning the sky. We were well aware of the war because of school programs for recycling paper, tin cans, and rubber. At the grocery store, rationing stamps were needed to buy sugar and other scarce items.

And, of course since China was under attack by the Japanese, my parents had a strong interest in war developments as they both had relatives still in Hoi Ping. Father sent money regularly to help his family in China during the war.

Figure 15 John, George, Mary, and Eugenia c. 1945

Knowing only a few words of English, and unacquainted with the local customs, Quan Shee lived a very solitary life in Macon for the over 20 years that she lived there. She had no source of advice, information, or emotional support for critical matters such as her health, especially during pregnancies. Nor did she have any one to provide guidance or assistance in child rearing. The only other adult speaker of Chinese in town was Father, and she had no adult females for companionship at all.[41]

At some point, she was given an American name, Grace, but otherwise not much assimilation occurred for her during these years in Macon. Father, who assumed the name, Frank, learned enough English to deal with customers and get by in matters of daily living, although he lacked much in the way of English reading and writing skills. In China, he had obtained the equivalent of a 7th grade education, and was literate in Chinese, but it was of no value to him living in Georgia other than to enable him to read Chinese newspapers which were mailed from Chicago or San Francisco. Of course, this connection was vital for our parents to learn about events occurring in China, as well as issues relevant to Chinese in America.

Where and How We Lived

We did not live in a conventional dwelling like a house or apartment in a residential area as most everyone else did. Our laundry was located right in the middle of downtown Macon. Our street ran parallel to the main shopping street, Cherry, only a block away. Unlike people who lived in houses, we had no shady trees sheltering a grassy lawn or a front porch in front of our living quarters. We lived directly above the laundry in two large rooms, each about 20 feet wide and 25 feet deep. The front room faced Mulberry Street, a wide street with a park median about 20 feet wide that ran down the middle between the traffic going in opposite directions. From this second story vantage

---

[41] In 1930, there were only 72 female and 181 male Chinese in all of Georgia, the southern state with the most Chinese after Mississippi. Statistical Abstract of the United States. (U. S. Government Printing Office,1930).

point, we could watch the world go by below from one of three windows that looked down on Mulberry Street.

This front room looked out at the tall elm trees that separated the east and west sides of the street. In the summer we would sometimes go during the hottest part of the afternoon and sit on the grass under these tall shade trees to cool off.

During the fall, parades would be held along downtown streets whenever the local white high school had a football game. First, a marching band from the high school would lead the parade, followed by cars containing local celebrities or politicians. Sometimes, at the end of the parade, the band from the high school for blacks would appear. Their band was always more spirited and flashy than the band from the white high school, especially the drum major who was very dramatic in catching his baton behind his back after tossing it about 15 feet or more into the sky.

The three windows in the back room of our living space above the laundry looked out on the back parking lot of the Standard Oil filling station that was located at the south end of our block. The view extended farther, across an alley, to the back parking lot of the Christ Episcopal Church parish house.

A narrow corridor or hall about 6 feet wide separated our two symmetrical rooms, the front one facing west where my parents and sisters slept and the back room facing east where my brother and I slept on one side and where we cooked and ate meals on the other side. At the north end of the hall were two doors, one on the west side leading down to the front entrance on Mulberry Street and one on the east side leading directly into the back of the laundry.

This was an immensely practical living arrangement. No commuting was needed, and since we had no automobile, that was especially advantageous. For meals, we could run upstairs and eat, and then go back downstairs to work or mind the storefront.

Figure 16 Mulberry Street looking northwest from Third Street in 1953. Our laundry cannot be seen but it is just before the Lanier Hotel on the right side. The Confederate soldier monument is in the middle of the intersection at Second Street.

Our living quarters above the laundry were primitive, as they were probably originally designed to serve mainly as storage or office space rather than as a residence. Although there was a sink and a faucet with running water in an alcove of the back room, there was only cold water. We had to boil water if we wanted it hot. We had no toilet in our living area. To use a flush toilet, we had to go downstairs back into the laundry where there was a toilet enclosed in a small booth located near the pressing machines.

We avoided using the toilet at night, if at all possible. First of all, the laundry was dark then and you had to take a flashlight to grope your way through the work area of laundry equipment. It was also unpleasant because huge cockroaches came out at night, so you tried to do your 'business' quickly. Roaches were disgusting, especially if you squished one by stepping on it, but at least they didn't bite or sting. Going to the toilet at night was definitely not an appealing thought.

In fact, when we were small children we were allowed to do our toilet stuff upstairs. A galvanized pail, strategically placed behind a curtain in the alcove of the back room near the sink, served as the toilet for us children. Periodically, when the pail was almost full, Mother had the chore of hauling it down the back stairs that led directly into the laundry where she could empty the contents into a real flush toilet. It was not a pleasant chore, as the stench of the urine was strong and the pail was nearly full so she had to be strong but also careful not to spill the contents on her journey. At least for us boys, up to the age of probably 3, we were taught to place some newspaper on the hallway floor, squat, and did what we had to do. Then we called Mother to clean it up!

Nor did we have a shower or bathtub. We would wash ourselves with wet towels, but usually we tried to avoid this ordeal. Mother would boil water in a kettle and pour it into a galvanized tub about two feet wide if she needed hot water for us to wash our feet at bedtime. A footbath was particularly needed in the summer for us boys, as we would spend most of the time running around in bare feet until we were six or seven.

We had no real furniture or items designed and sold as furniture, aside from our beds, several old wooden chairs, and a kitchen table. For everything else we improvised, adapting orange or apple crates and other wood boxes for makeshift use as stands and storage units.

Another part of the large room served as both the kitchen and as an eating area. It contained two gas burners on a stand and a refrigerator. Meal preparation was done on a wood kitchen table, which doubled as a serving table where we ate our meals. In the corner facing one of the back windows was a large sink for washing dishes, pots, and pans.

I recall that when I was not yet in school, there was a pot bellied stove near the eating area that burned coal. We would toss small lumps of coal from a mound of coal stacked next to it into the stove, close its door, and huddle close to get warm.

By the time I started school, I think the coal stove was no longer there. We had no heating system then aside from a small gas heater about two feet wide and a foot high. In the winter, we slept under very heavy Chinese cotton quilts that were very warm and cozy once we got acclimated to the ice-cold sheets. As children, we could barely move under the weight of the quilts. When we got up in the morning, Mother would start the gas heater before we awoke. We would then rush from the bed over to the heater and crouch in front of it to get warmed up for five or ten minutes before we could bear to eat breakfast or do anything else to get ready to go to school.

When we got older, Father got some wallboard and constructed 6 foot high 'walls,' really room dividers, partitioning the two rooms in half, creating four rooms and affording more privacy for everyone. Now my parents had a 'room,' my sisters had one, and George and I had one. The fourth area served as the kitchen and eating area.

Living In Downtown Macon

When I speak of downtown, I really mean the commercial or business section of Macon, because Macon was not a very large city. We spent all of our time, work or leisure, in the downtown area because we never had occasion to visit the outlying and suburban areas. The town was small enough to go on foot to any place we needed to buy food, to buy clothing, or to see "picture shows," as people in the South called movies. In any case, we had no automobile and neither my Father nor Mother knew how to drive. Besides, we did not know anyone who lived outside the main business area to visit anyway. We really had no neighboring families with children near us that we could play with.

Downtown included roughly nine square blocks lying between Walnut Street on the east and Poplar Street on the west, First Street on the north, and to the south, Broadway (renamed Martin Luther King Boulevard following the civil rights revolution of the 1960s). As the "Harlem" of Macon, this street served as the gathering place of social life for black people. There were eating places, some bars, liquor stores, and a few cheap retail stores. The Douglass Theater[42] was the only place in this segregated town where blacks could see a movie. This theater had a rich association with live music performances by celebrated Negro singers and musicians, as Bessie Smith had performed there in the 1920s. In the 1950s and later, influential black rock and roll musicians from the area such as Little Richard, Otis Redding, and James Brown performed live concerts there. With the social changes following civil rights laws dramatically improving the status of blacks during the 1960s, this 'colored-only' theatre closed. Many years later, the Douglass was refurbished and resurrected, and became an entertainment center for the entire city.

In marked contrast to other parts of downtown, where the streets were generally sparsely populated, Broadway was full of activity. On Saturday afternoons and evenings especially, Broadway was teeming with social life for many black people. Due to the heat and nonexistent air conditioning in the summer, people just stood around on the sidewalk and socialized. Some would become intoxicated, and fights would sometimes arise. There were always police officers patrolling the area, with the paddy wagon stationed close at hand. It was a scary area for a small child. Sometimes I went there with Father when we were short-handed in the laundry due to absenteeism to look for temporary workers to hire for help in the laundry.

Within the downtown area were retail stores such as Davidson's department store, J. C. Penney's, and several 5 and 10-cent chain stores

---

[42] The name of the theater has no relation to Frederick Douglass, the former slave who was the leading black abolitionist of the 19th century

such as Woolworth, Kress, W. T. Grant, Silvers, and J. J. Newberry. These stores were favorite hangouts for us kids. We would look for inexpensive toys there as well as all of our supplies for school. Mother also shopped in them for most of her household needs because they were the least expensive stores. I would often spend an hour or two going through all five of the local 5 and 10-cent stores, all located within several blocks and just a short walk away from home.

Figure 17 Looking south on Cherry Street, the downtown shopping area in 1953.

I especially loved to go to the Kress store at the north end of our main street, Cherry. First, as I entered the store, I perused the long candy counter, which displayed a huge assortment of goodies in different bins behind glass for me to drool over. Next I looked at the school supplies before heading to the toy counter where I would linger over the toys, playing with items if the sales clerk did not object. When

I was about 8, I discovered that if I bought a coloring book or toy from one particular sales clerk, she would surreptitiously slip my dime or quarter into the bag containing my purchase. I never mentioned this anomaly to anyone, and I must confess that I always looked for her whenever I wanted to make a purchase. At the back of the store I would admire the hundreds of goldfish for sale in the big tank. I was fascinated watching them dart in and out among the many fish crammed in the tank. Eventually I persuaded Mother to let us have a few fish.

Finally, I was ready to leave Kress, which was the nicest dime store in town and head out into the hot outdoors to visit the other dime stores. Before leaving to go face the heat outside, I would stop and drink from the drinking fountain, because the coldest water in town was at Kress! There were separate drinking fountains marked 'White' and 'Colored,' but when we were very young, we were not sure which one to use. If whites saw us drinking from the 'Colored' fountain, some directed us to use the white facilities.

Next, along my route, I would move to the next block to browse through Woolworth's, which usually did not have much of interest. At the next corner was another five and dime store, J. J. Newberry's, which had a basement where the toys were displayed. At Third Street, I would swing to the right and cross the street to Silver's dime store and then double back through W. T. Grant's. By then I was ready to head home, two blocks away. There were no more stores that would interest a child. Often I did not have a cent to spend, but I had a fine time just looking at and handling the toys.

Just after the war, we noticed that many items, especially toys, from Japan flooded the stores. They were all marked underneath as 'Made in Occupied Japan.' Because Japan had aggressed against China, I avoided buying them. In those days, unlike today, those toys had the reputation of being inferior plastic items or cheap imitations of American toys.

A couple of blocks from our laundry there were two large chain grocery stores where Mother did most of her food shopping, a Piggly Wiggly and a Great Atlantic & Pacific store. The movie theatres were among the few air-conditioned establishments in that day so they were a welcome refuge on hot summer afternoons. On really oppressive days, we would stay in the theater and watch the movie twice to avoid having to face the humid and hot air outside. Scattered in between the clothing, jewelry, and other retail shops were a few restaurants, several hotels, two 10 to 15-story office buildings (tall, for Macon), and the usual assortment of barbers, drug stores, furniture stores, and banks.

On the block where we lived, the Lanier Hotel stood several storefronts away. I loved going through its revolving glass door entrance, the only one I had ever encountered. I spent a lot of my spare time in the lobby because it had a newspaper and magazine stand that sold candy and comic books. That is where I bought a lot of candy like Hershey Bars and Tootsie Rolls. I would hide in the corner behind some of the magazine racks where I would not be noticed by the clerk so I could read the comic books without having to buy any. Some of the clerks did not care while others asked me to stop reading the comics unless I was buying some. So, I would read as many as I could in a few minutes and then I would buy an issue of one of my favorite comics like *Superman* or *Batman* to appease the clerk. I also liked to read the ones Jean would buy such as *Looney Toons, Little Lulu,* or *Wonder Woman* but she did not seem to care for my selections.

Beyond the hotel at the corner of Mulberry and Second Streets, a Confederate soldier monument sat squarely on a small mound in the middle of the intersection. The Confederacy is a strong southern icon, revered by some but rejected as outdated or frivolous by others.[43] In public school, we often sang "Bonnie Blue Flag," a song that was the equivalent of the national anthem for the Confederacy. One of the lines is, "And when our rights were threatened, the cry rose near and far, Hurrah for the Bonnie Blue Flag." Even Southerners who disagree with the racial prejudices of the old South will still rally to defend other southern values against Yankee carpetbaggers. And, of course, in school we also often sang "Dixie." Because of their association with the Jim Crow segregation traditions, with the civil rights activism of the 1960s both of these songs became as politically unacceptable as Confederate flags were.

Opposite the Confederate-soldier monument stood the Bibb Country courthouse, a four-story, rock-solid imposing building with its crowning dome that had a huge clock on all four sides that tolled out the hour in solemn tones throughout the day and night. Next to it

[43]The Confederate soldier monument was in the middle of the intersection of Mulberry and Second Streets in 1953 (see Figure 16) as it was back in 1906 (see left side of Figure 19). But when I visited in 2003, left turn lanes had displaced the statue, now relegated to a site where it did not impede traffic.

stood the Grand Theater, where grand opera had once been staged. It was Macon's finest movie theater showing only first-run films, and in 1945 it held the world premiere of "God is my co-pilot" which celebrated a hometown hero, Colonel Robert Lee Scott who fought against the Japanese with the famed "Flying Tigers" squadron. It was such a big event that a parade preceded the film showing.

There were several public buildings that especially impressed us children. At the foot of Cherry Street stood the grand railroad terminal with its high vaulted ceiling and marble floors. When trains were about to depart, an announcer would blare out on a loudspeaker, but in a muffled and unintelligible mumble, the stops along the route of each train and its departure track.

The post office, one block south of us on Mulberry Street was built in the typical style of 1920s federal buildings. Constructed with white granite, it was very stately in appearance. We were fascinated when we saw all the 'Wanted' posters of fugitives displayed next to the postal boxes.

Several blocks to the north of our laundry, Mulberry Street abruptly ended where it ran into Spring Street. This was at the foot of Coleman Hill, a park situated on a bluff that overlooked the downtown part of the city. Across from the park to the right was Whittle School, which all of us children attended. Since it was only four blocks away, we were able to walk to and from school in about 10 to 15 minutes.

Our Schooling

Success in school was strongly encouraged by my parents as

they realized that education was the key to getting ahead. A surefire excuse to get out of doing work in the laundry was having school homework to complete.

We children started school with a disadvantage because we learned to speak Chinese before we learned English, which was not surprising since our parents spoke only Chinese to us when we were small. The little English I knew by the time I started school was what I learned from talking with my older sisters and customers in the laundry. Until we entered school, our opportunity to learn much about the world outside the laundry was very limited.

I did not know much about how Mary liked school, but Jean and I enjoyed it and did well. We were excellent students, so we managed to be very popular with our teachers and our parents were very pleased. School and learning were our passports to success. We enjoyed many hours exploring knowledge through the seemingly endless supply of books that we could borrow from the public library. Without this facility, it is unlikely that we would have been so academically successful.

My younger brother, George, was someone who would today be termed "developmentally disabled." Mother did the best she could to manage him, but nothing seemed to help. She became increasingly protective of George, which is understandable. At the same time, George learned to be dependent on this treatment and it prevented him from developing many skills within his capability. Thus, even though he did not make much effort at learning to read in school, he did learn to read movie ads in the newspaper, and to a limited degree, material on other topics that interested him.

School was fun and I enjoyed learning. I liked all of my teachers, looking up to them as mother figures, I guess. In return, they all seemed to like me because I was well behaved in addition to being very studious and intelligent. I was able to stand out academically in spite of disadvantages of growing up in a home where English was not spoken, perhaps because my classmates came from working class backgrounds and had parents with little education.

Each morning we started the school day by standing and dutifully reciting the Pledge of Allegiance as we faced the American flag with our right hands across our hearts. We then sat down, closed our eyes, placed our hands together, and recited the Lord's Prayer before any school lessons began. In first grade, I quickly learned to read using the old *Dick and Jane* readers (*See Dick run. Run Dick run*). Although I excelled in English skills such as reading and writing in school, I was still literal-minded in my comprehension of the language. Thus, I vividly recall one time when I was in the second or third grade our teacher told us that spring was coming, and that we should look for 'signs' of spring. I did not know that a sign could be a figure of speech so I imagined there were man-made signs posted along roads and streets that, in effect, proclaimed 'spring is coming.' I was distressed the next day because many children raised their hands when the teacher asked how many had noticed 'signs' of spring as I had not been able to find a single one.

In third grade, I was selected to be one of the two representatives for the school in the countywide spelling bee, an exciting event especially since it was broadcast live over the radio. We had listened to it at home every year, and rooted for the students from our school. Now I was pretty good in spelling, and I won Third Place that year. I misspelled 'develop' by adding an *e* at the end. I was disappointed because it was such a simple word to miss. A nice teacher at another school wrote me an encouraging letter, claiming that she had always spelled it with an *e* at the end as well.

One example of the supportive influence of my elementary school teachers involved the time when I sustained a first-degree burn on the back of my right hand because a worker I was helping accidentally closed a shirt-pressing machine on it. My hand was bandaged for several months and the burn left a gruesome-looking scar that I still bear.

I was entering sixth grade and until then I had a perfect grade record since first grade. I had always received E's (for Excellent) in every category that we got graded on. Instead of worrying about the condition of my hand, all I could think of was receiving lower grades for penmanship because my written schoolwork looked terrible as I struggled to write with my left hand. I resigned myself to getting a marginally passing grade for penmanship and was quite surprised and elated when Mrs. Mincey, my sixth grade teacher still gave me a grade of E in writing.

Another example of her understanding and compassion came when we had class elections. I was nominated for President, but lost handily to a more popular student. I was embarrassed as well as disappointed, but Mrs. Mincey took me aside to console me. She reassured me that the class had based its vote on popularity and that I should have been elected on merit.

In our elementary schools, we had visiting or roving teachers for special topics. Thus, once a month or so, an art teacher came to visit our class to give a drawing 'lesson,' which consisted of little more than giving us a nice sheet of drawing paper and free time to use our crayons to create any picture that we could make.

The head coach for the boys' high school football and basketball teams, Selby Buck, came to our school about once a month to teach the boys some fundamental skills related to these sports. This was rather exciting, because we admired and supported the high school athletic teams, even though they had a meek nickname, "Poets," because the school was named after Sidney Lanier, a famous local poet from the Civil war era (referred to only as the "War Between the States" by Southerners). Nevertheless, we were thrilled that their coach came to our school in person to teach us how to throw or catch a football.

For music education, the specialist teacher did not actually visit to each school in person. Instead, she had a weekly radio broadcast that our class listened to at school. She discussed the background of a classical composer and then played some of his music after which our regular teacher tried without much success to involve us in some discussion about the music.

In addition, sometime near the end of the school day, our teachers might play the piano to accompany our singing. Many of the songs, I seem to recall, had Southern roots. There were the Stephen

Foster classics like *Old Folks At Home, My Old Kentucky Home, Old Black Joe,* and of course, *Camptown Races.* There were even a few Negro spiritual songs like *Nobody Knows The Trouble I've Seen.*

And, of course, it was always rousing to belt out the defiant chorus to *Dixie,* the unofficial anthem of the South.

Then I wish I was in Dixie, hooray! Hooray!

In Dixie land I'll take my stand, to live and die in Dixie,

Away, away, away down south in Dixie,

Away, away, away down south in Dixie.

As a young child I did not understand the deeper socially divisive issues underlying these lyrics. I simply viewed it as a statement expressing the loyalty and pride that we southerners had for our region of the country.

The Public Library

The Washington Memorial Library, located about 10 long blocks away, was a magical and transforming place for me. I remember my first visit there as if it happened yesterday. It was on a summer afternoon, when I was probably about 5 and had not yet started school. I was playing alone in the alley that ran between the yard behind our laundry and the grounds behind the Christ Church when I spotted my sisters. They told me they were headed for the public library, a place I had never heard of, but they allowed me to tag along.

Before I started school, I had some familiarity with books as my parents did have in their possession some dozen or so elementary school level readers. I never learned how my parents came to have these books since they could not read English. I would pester Jean to read them to me before I started learning to read in school. I especially enjoyed one on Aesop's fables, complete with illustrations. In addition, some of the laundry customers who took an interest in broadening our contact with great literature made gifts to us of classic children's stories like *Treasure Island, Robinson Crusoe,* and *Gulliver's Travels* with color illustrations at Christmas time.

However, seeing the sheer size of the public library collection I was overwhelmed. Never had I ever seen so many books, and I soon resolved to read all of them. I began my lifelong love of books and became a frequent book borrower. The trek to the library was a slow, tiring walk when carrying an armful of books especially during the hot summer days. The last block led through a lovely park to a steep set of stairs that ended at the crest of the hill upon which the library stood. But the trip was well worth it, as the treasures within opened the world of literature and knowledge to me. Books were my inspiration, and opened a much wider and richer world to me.

Our Church "Playground"

We did not belong to or attend any church, although my sisters did sometimes go with classmates to Sunday school at a Methodist church. Nonetheless, the Christ Episcopal Church, which was conveniently located just beyond our back yard, was more important to us because its grounds served as a wonderful place for us to play when we were young.

We readily imagined the church buildings, with a tower, bell, turrets, breezeway, courtyard, and gardens to be medieval forts, castles, or palaces. Most days, aside from Sundays, it was deserted, and we played "hide and go seek," "Mother, may I," and games pitting cowboys versus Indians in the narrow passages, nooks, and crannies between the buildings, on the spacious front lawn, and in the gated garden that sat alongside the breezeway connecting the parish house with the sanctuary.

Not knowing any better, I would sometimes break off small branches of trees and bushes and then strip the bark to made a bow and a set of arrows. I would pretend I was Robin Hood and shoot at targets on a wall, but I was not too skilled and soon lost interest. Fortunately, I was never caught doing this unwitting vandalism.

Figure 18   Our personal 'playground' behind Christ Church.

We did not have any park nearby with play equipment but we managed to have lots of fun playing our own games on the grounds of the church. I made friends with the janitor, Willie, and we never had any problems playing on the grounds as long as we were quiet whenever church functions were being held. Mr. Willingham, a successful merchant and church elder, donated the basketball goal. He was always very cordial toward me. Luckily for me, no one ever used it so I had the goal all for myself. I would create two all-star teams of my favorite players, and pretend I was each of them as I took shots at the goal for them during fantasy games.

Our Backyard "Farm"

One day Father decided he would raise chickens in the yard behind the laundry along with the Chinese vegetables he was growing. He took me down the street to a feed store that sold baby chicks and we bought a dozen or more that day. Father had already built a chicken coop to house them at night. We enjoyed looking at and feeding the chicks. When they matured, we harvested a small supply of eggs, but the main goal was to have fresh homegrown chicken to serve for Sunday dinner. This was not a pleasant topic for us children, as we quickly became attached to the birds, dumb as they were. Actually, we lost more than a few to rats who killed them at night. We also had several roosters, pretty ornery ones that would chase us when we approached the chickens. I don't know whether Mother made soup out of the roosters since they are rather tough, but I do recall sadly that my favorite hen, named Brownie because of the color of her feathers, was the last chicken of the lot to survive before she too was served up for dinner, a meal of which I did not partake.

Those chickens were the only ones we raised. We found it was far easier to go to the market on Saturday, buy a grown chicken, and bring it home for Mother to slaughter for Sunday dinner. And it was much less emotionally wearing. My parents continued their vegetable garden, but the only crop that seemed to flourish was aptly named, bitter melon (*foo gwah*). It is a shiny green, pebbled squash that tasted awful to me and I never was able to acquire a liking for it.

Our Pets

We never had any pets, unless goldfish or little turtles purchased at the Kress five-and-ten cent store count, because Mother objected to furry pets which she felt were dirty or spreaders of disease. Our water pets would usually die in the unbearable summer heat, even though we changed their water frequently. We did have a stray cat that hung around our yard; she gave birth to a litter of about 6 kittens that we adopted as outdoor pets but as they matured, they wandered off.

The neighbors' animals served as our pets: a gray tabby from Wright's Seed Store next door, Timmy, was very friendly. He came out each morning and we would play with him for a while. My friend, Felton, who lived in a boarding house run by his mother on the other side of the block next to the Christ Church, had a mutt named Fuzzy who was fun to play with. We never could teach him any tricks, which was probably more a reflection on our ineptitude rather than on Fuzzy's mental capacity. Actually, we did have a puppy, but only for less than a month. My sister Jean and I had somehow finally persuaded

Mother to let us get a dog from the pound. As both Jean and I were inexperienced with dogs and frightened by the larger or louder ones, we picked the smallest and most docile puppy in the pound. Mostly white, with some black and brown spots, we named him Butchie, don't ask me why, and took him home. At bedtime we put him in a enclosure that proved to be too loose, and then one morning he was gone. Sadly, we never saw him again. That was the last of Butchie, but I'm sure Mother was relieved.

What and How We Ate

While we were growing up in Macon, we never once ate at a restaurant. When I was a child, in fact, I don't think I even understood what a restaurant was. Mother cooked all the family meals every day except on Saturdays when all of us were so busy working in the laundry. We did not actually wash nor iron on Saturdays, which was a day off for the workers. But it was payday for most of our customers and so the most popular day to pick up clean clothes for going out Saturday night and attending church on Sunday.

This meant Mother had no time to cook lunch, so I was delegated to run over to the nearby Krystal hamburger diner, in those days the equivalent of MacDonald's. It was fascinating for me to watch the cook flip burgers on the grill situated at the front of the store just beyond the front counter. He cleaned the grill, slapped down several rows of about 8 or more patties in each row, and shortly afterwards flipped them over in quick succession. Cooking the meat patties, adding the buns, and then packaging the burgers in cardboard wrappers all had to be done rapidly to keep up with the many orders.

In the South, where work tended to proceed at a snail's pace it was exciting to observe the rapid pace of hamburger production at Krystal's.

I would order a dozen burgers, all of which were rather small, and bring them back to the laundry for us to eat during breaks between customers. That was my only encounter with any type of American food aside from what the school cafeteria served for lunch. There, we were exposed to foods like cole slaw, grapefruit juice, and corn bread. We much preferred Chinese cooking, but of course it was an unfair comparison. School lunches are not representative of American cooking, but we did not know that when we were children.

Basically, Mother's cooking involved what is called stir-fry, although she also made some stews and Chinese-style soups. We assumed everyone cooked with a wok over a flaming gas stove. She adapted her cooking style to local foods such as collard greens, okra, and turnips and cooked them Chinese style, using high flames to quickly sauté the food so it was firm rather than limp from being overcooked. She never used a cookbook or a written recipe since she did everything from memory, or instinct, or improvisation. She invented her own stews, incorporating various combinations of available ingredients. When she later gave me tips on cooking, it was entirely a matter of watching and remembering what she did. I can't recall ever seeing Father cook a single time while we were growing up, but he must have known how or else he taught himself quickly, because during the summer of 1953 when he and I were alone there, as will be explained later, he cooked our meals and gave me some tips on the correct way to cook rice, slice flank steak, and stir fry it with various vegetables.

Mother's dishes were not the kind of fare typically found in Chinese restaurants. We never heard of chow mein, fried rice, egg rolls, sweet and sour pork, egg foo young, and other dishes popular with white customers of Chinese restaurants. Nor did we get to enjoy authentic delicacies like Peking duck or shark's fin soup from China favored by Chinese patrons. It was not until years later after we moved to San Francisco that we ever ate in a Chinese restaurant. Instead we were treated to calf brain soup, pig stomach, and other dishes that are not served in most Chinese restaurants. Although they might not sound appealing to those who never ate them, we loved these home-cooked dishes because we grew up eating them regularly.

We were able occasionally to purchase fresh Chinese vegetables like bok choy and winter melon delivered by truck from farms in Florida that shipped directly to us. My parents ordered many food ingredients that would have been impossible to find in Georgia by mail from Chinese merchants in San Francisco. These foods often came from China in a dried or preserved form such as black mushrooms, dried turnips, lily roots, translucent noodles called sai fun, and fermented bean curd. I was fascinated that when these shriveled items were soaked in water for a short time they would be restored to their original condition so they could be cooked. In addition, they bought cans and bottles of Chinese spices and sauces, especially soy, black bean, and hoisin. One of my favorite items was fermented bean curd cakes that we ate with fresh stir fried spinach. Sometimes there would be Chinese candies and other snacks like dried lichee nuts and salted preserved plums (moi) for us children, which we would fight over.

We never ate desserts, as Mother never served any. We did not even know that American meals typically ended with a sweet. That is not to say that we never had sweet snacks. Aside from the grocery stores, the bakery was one food store that Mother sometimes frequented and where she would occasionally buy glazed donuts, ladyfingers, or lemon meringue pies. They were a great treat for us kids.

Our breakfasts sometimes resembled the American meal of eggs, bacon, and toast with jam but most of the time they were improvised. Mother was too busy to spend much time making breakfast on workday mornings. She sometimes cooked scrambled eggs, but that was probably the one dish that eluded her, as the eggs were either too oily or too dry. When we were very young, she made Cream of Wheat or Quaker Oats oatmeal for us on cold mornings. When we got old enough to go to school, we often fed ourselves dry cereals such as Rice Krispies or corn flakes with milk.

In the hot summers with sweltering 90 to 95 degree days and high humidity, cooking was especially unpleasant, but Mother never complained. She prepared and cooked every meal, every day, year in and year out, with only occasional help from Father on Sundays.

Mother had to go grocery shopping several days a week, because there was no way to keep food fresh with only a small refrigerator, and no freezer. She would shop when work was slow. In the summer that time fell in the middle of the day when the heat was the greatest. Without a car or cart, Mother had to carry one heavy sack of groceries under each arm several blocks from the Great A & P Market and the Piggly Wiggly grocery store back to the laundry.

During the workweek, we had to eat dinner in shifts. After Mother finished cooking about six in the evening, she would go back downstairs to serve any customers who wanted to pick up laundry while we children ate our meal. If it were not too busy in the laundry, Father would come upstairs and eat next while we tended the store and waited on customers. Then Father would go back to the laundry while Mother came up to eat, clean up and wash the dishes. Occasionally, our parents traded their shifts, but we children always got to eat first.

Sunday Dinners

We often had a special treat when Mother would buy a live chicken to prepare for Sunday lunch or dinner. On Saturday afternoon I would play with the chicken, which was cooped in a wooden crate. On Sunday morning, Mother would firmly grab the chicken by its feet with one hand. Then holding the chicken upside down over the sink and with a cleaver in her other hand, she would calmly and swiftly slit the chicken's throat as it flapped its wings furiously struggling. She would quickly shove the chicken, with blood gushing from its neck, into a metal pail and cover it with a lid. The chicken would flounder about for a few moments, its feet scratching frantically against the galvanized metal, before it expired. Then she would pluck the feathers and soon after, boil it. Probably, because I was allowed to observe this procedure from an early age, it never bothered me in the least. She never shielded me or prevented me from watching, nor did she ever discuss the process with me. It was just a normal routine as far as she was concerned.

When it was ready, Father would remove the chicken from the pot, and using a cleaver, chop the chicken into small pieces, which we dipped in soy sauce and hot mustard made from Colman's dry mustard powder. Mother would use the chicken broth to make a soup, with dried seaweed and dried shrimp, which we loved. Once in a while she would prepare a duck for Sunday dinner. Mother would make me a toy "drum" by taking the tough parchment-like duck skin and stretching it across an empty tin can from which both ends had been removed.

Sundays were special for many reasons. We got to sleep in late, as there was no school and no work. But perhaps the most important reason was that it was the one day in the week when our family could enjoy our special Sunday dinners with all of us together.

4. *Inside Sam Lee Laundry*

Our store, Sam Lee Laundry, was in the heart of downtown Macon on Mulberry Street near the Lanier Hotel, the second largest one in town. Directly across the park running down the middle of the street was the imposing Persons Building, an office building about 10 stories high. Between the hotel and our laundry was Wright's Seed Store. On the other side, a shoe repair shop operated until the end of the war when the Star Dry Cleaners opened there and took away some of our customers.

As a child, I wondered why our laundry had the name of someone other than my parents. They explained that there is no actual person named Sam Lee, but the name was used since 'family laundry' sounded like 'Sam Lee Laundry.' Apparently they were mistaken because I later learned that Sam Lee sounds like Chinese words for prosperity. Sam Lee was a popular business name, as if its use would bring good fortune from the laundry. In any case, "Sam Lee" was a popular name for Chinese laundries across the country. We never knew or even wondered exactly how old *our* Sam Lee Laundry was when we lived there.[44] Earlier Chinese operated it before Father bought it from them in 1928, but who they were and whether they might be related to us is unknown.[45] These Chinese may have either died or returned to China by the time my parents bought the laundry.

---

[44] Macon City Directory lists Sam Lee laundry at that same address as far back as 1888.

[45] The City Directory listed a "Yin Gee" as living with my parents at the 363 Cotton Ave. laundry office but only in 1930. My parents never mentioned him so it is unlikely he was a relative but my guess is that he sold one or both laundries to them and then returned to China.

Figure 19 Sam Lee Laundry in 1906 is to the right of the 4-story Lanier hotel. The three windows above looked out from our eventual living quarters. Courtesy, Georgia Archives.

Figure 20 Sam Lee Laundry in 1953 was in the same building it occupied in 1906.

Even with this documented history of our laundry, this evidence did not have any emotional impact on me. An old saying attributed to the Chinese is that a picture is worth 1,000 words. Its truth was never more apparent to me than when many years later I found visual evidence of the 1906 existence of the two-story building where my family lived and worked from 1928 to 1956.

A comparison of Figures 19 and 20 reveals a store sign hanging outside the middle of three windows on the second level above the laundry. It is very likely the same sign in both photographs, but with fresher paint in 1953 when I recall seeing, 'Sam Lee Laundry' on it in white letters against a red background.

Sam Lee Laundry had a wide storefront, about 20 feet, in comparison to some of the small Chinese laundries I later saw across the country that were mere 'hole-in-the-wall' stores. It was also deep, extending over 100 feet from the front to the back door. Upon entering the store, a 6 x 20 foot customer waiting area led up to the front counter that separated customers from the laundry work area.

Off to the left side of the customer area was a changing room for male customers who needed their trousers steam pressed while they waited. On the left front side of the store behind the front counter, wrapped packages of finished laundry were stacked on several shelves for pickup. Behind this was a large worktable about 15 feet long used for sorting finished laundry into different piles for each customer. Every item that belonged to a customer had to be located before all of it would be packaged in brown paper. Then Father would total the price for all of the items, write the sum on the ticket, and the package would be stacked on a shelf with the other packages. We did not have a cash register but used a cash drawer. When closed, it was locked shut unless you pulled the correct combination of levers that were hidden under it.

Father had learned from equipment salesmen after the war that more money could be made with dry cleaning than in washing clothes, so he purchased their equipment and quickly learned how to offer these services. The finished garments were placed in brown paper garment bags. The right side of the store behind the front counter was reorganized to serve for hanging cleaned garments awaiting pickup. Father fashioned two levels of racks using galvanized pipes. To retrieve garments from the higher rack that was about eight feet above the ground, he improvised a tool by hammering a nail at a 45-degree angle into the end of a six-foot round wooden pole. First, we would reach up and shove the improvised hook at the end of the pole under the curve of the coat hanger. Then we pushed it up about an inch to clear the pipe. And then we would swing the suspended garments in an downward arc to bring them within reach in the same motion. Finally, we would grab hold of the top of the hanger that held the garments. This operation avoided the need for a stepladder so even we children usually could manage it, but sometimes the garments were too heavy for us, and we dropped them. This was embarrassing, but fortunately, we were far enough behind the front counter that customers usually did not witness our clumsiness.

Off to the right side behind the front counter was Mother's Singer treadle sewing machine with which she mended clothes and sewed military insignia onto the sleeves of the shirts and jackets of soldiers stationed nearby during the war. When Mother was not using it and allowed us to, we loved to play with it, piercing holes in paper that we pretended to be sewing as we pedaled furiously on the treadle.[46]

Located in the middle of the laundry were two large washing machines, each about 4 or 5 feet in diameter, and about 6 to 8 feet in length. Into one went light-colored and white clothing and bed linens; into the other went dark and usually grimier clothing. Many of our customers were laborers whose work clothes were greasy and dirty. In the morning, Father would fill the big washers with clothes, add soap, and sometimes bluing, and run a wash. Nearby the several hand-cranked wringers squeezed out excess water left when the clothes were removed from the washers. Adjacent to the wringers were two large wooden sinks where he starched some items such as shirt collars. In addition, there was a machine called an extractor, which had an inner round perforated drum about three feet in diameter. When it spun rapidly, like a centrifuge, it removed excess water from items that had just been washed so they could be readily ironed.

Off in another section were the dry cleaning machine and a steam-pressing machine used expressly for dry cleaned garments. In the farther rear of the store were four or five steam-pressing machines used to iron trousers, underwear, and sheets, and several shirt-pressing machines designed specifically to iron, and fold, white business shirts quickly.

---

[46] Although she had little 'free time,' Mother used it to sew many of her own clothes.

74

LAUNDRY & CLEANING
MACHINERY & ACCESSORIES
489 Courtland St., N. E.   AT. 3806
ATLANTA, GEORGIA

Figure 21 Ad for a shirt pressing machine like the ones Father purchased in 1950.

A single toilet stall stood in the middle of this laundry equipment. The half dozen women who worked in the laundry vied with us for its use. We never had a feeling of privacy because the workers were pressing clothes just outside the enclosure. When it was occupied for a long time, and nature's calls were urgent, I used to run down to the corner Standard Oil filling station and sneak into their public toilet. Besides, their toilet was cleaner, and a lot less overheated during the summer, than ours!

In one corner of this machinery section, off to one side, was a staircase leading directly to our living area. At one time, you entered these back stairs from outside the laundry, but when I was about 5 or 6, an extension of about 50 feet was added to the rear of the building to house more laundry equipment and the dry cleaning machine and steam presser. At that point, the rear staircase that had opened into the back yard became enclosed within the laundry.

Next to the stairs, perched up on a wooden stand about four feet high sat a large round water tank, probably about six feet high and five feet in diameter. I never understood why this storage tank was needed in the operation of the laundry. However, what was special about it to me was that one summer Father installed a bypass from this water tank to make us a shower. Since the water was not heated, we could not use it to shower most of the year, but it was wonderfully delightful in the hot, muggy, summer months.

On workdays during the humid and hot summer days, we survived by drinking ice water all day, provided the ice wagon came. A black man would drive his horse-drawn wagon carrying large blocks of ice up Mulberry Street past the laundry every working day around mid-morning. For 5 or 10 cents, you could buy a large block of ice to put in a water cooler and it would last several hours. On weekends, or days when the ice wagon passed us by because we did not run out to order in time, we just suffered with the heat. Our other main source of liquid nourishment was ice cold Coca Cola, the unofficial soft drink of the South, which we would get from the vending machine at the corner Standard Oil filling station.

The summer heat was so oppressive that we tried to exert as little effort as possible and still get the chores done. In those days, air conditioning was not available except in picture show theatres and large department stores. All we had to cool off with were two large electric fans in the front of the laundry that gave a bit of respite. Upstairs, we relied on two oscillating electric fans and one window exhaust fan to circulate the hot, humid air.

One thing that always puzzled me was the sign in front of our laundry. It read "hand laundry," but every washing and ironing operation was done by machine. However, earlier in its history, it had truly been a hand laundry. After hand washing in a tub or on a metal board, clothes were ironed with heavy hand irons that were heated on a coal stove. Water sprayed from brass misting cans served to dampen clothes before ironing them. But by the time I was growing up, mechanical drum washers and steam pressing machines had made these devices obsolete, but I recall seeing them abandoned in the store.

Customers usually addressed Father as Sam or Sam Lee because that was the name on the sign hanging in front of the store. Few customers knew his American name was actually Frank Jung, and most of them would not address him with the same respect they would use in addressing a white person by greeting him as "Mr. Jung," even if they knew his American name.

When I visited the several Chinese laundries operating in Atlanta in the 1940s, I noticed that our laundry was much larger and more modern than the little laundries with antiquated equipment that many other Chinese had. What struck and puzzled me was the iron bars, about 3 or 4 inches apart, that ran from the front counter top up to near the ceiling, similar to those that separated customers from tellers at banks of that era. A small opening between some of the bars enabled the laundryman and the customer to exchange goods and money. These barriers served to protect the laundryman, often the sole occupant of the store, from assault and robbery. In contrast, the front section of our laundry was open, with a 10-15 foot wide waist-high counter extending across the storefront. Customers did not line up single file but could await service along the entire counter front.

Father did the sorting, marking, inventory, and washing of the laundry items. Sometimes my sisters would help with the sorting and inventorying of incoming laundry from customers. Five or six black women, of varying ages, did the ironing and pressing: shirts, pants, overalls, towels, sheets, and everything else that needed to be done. Most of these women were illiterate, but this did not pose a problem for their job since they did not interact with customers dropping off or picking up laundry.

In the 1940s our worker wages were as low as between one and two dollars per *day*, which they received at the end of the week. Absenteeism among workers was common on Mondays. Turnover was frequent, some workers lasting only a few weeks. This unreliable workforce created an added burden for my parents who had to take up the slack. In addition, Father had to take time from doing his work to go search for these women where they lived to urge them to come to work. He could not phone them as most of them could not afford telephones; besides we did not have one either until about 1948.

When customers brought in dirty, and often foul-smelling, laundry, we issued a ticket to them. We put their items together in a packet until each item was inventoried and given identification marks or tags. Usually the customer's initials or some unique combination of letters were indelibly inked onto an inconspicuous part of the item such as the inside back of trouser pockets or the inside back of shirt collars so that after the laundry for a given wash load was done we could combine the items that belonged to each customer into a single package.

White-collar workers gave us easier, 'cleaner' laundry but most of our customers, blue-collar workers and laborers, brought in grimy, greasy, stained, and filthy clothes and overalls. We children held our breath and noses when we had to handle this foul-smelling laundry. The customers were fairly evenly split between whites and blacks, except during the war in the early 1940s when we got business from many soldiers, all white, from a nearby military base, Camp Wheeler and Warner Robbins Air Force Base.

Laundry items were usually washed on Monday and Wednesday mornings, and ironed in the afternoon or the next day. The day after laundering was complete, Father sorted the finished items to gather all of the items that each customer had brought in. This sorting required a good memory of where earlier items for each customer had been placed on the worktable. When the stack of laundry items for a customer matched the inventory, it was removed from the sorting table for wrapping, freeing space to start the assembly of items for another customer.

Then Father calculated on his abacus[47] the amount of the bill. During the years right after the war, we charged 12 cents to launder business shirts, 25 cents for a pair of pants and 35 cents for a pair of

---

[47] The abacus, an ancient Chinese device, fascinated us as well as the customers. Father used it as an adding machine (it is used for other arithmetic functions as well). The typical abacus has a wood frame about 8 inches high and 12 inches wide, with about a dozen parallel columns of movable round beads about the size and shape of Life Saver candies. Each column holds a stack of 5 beads below and two beads above a horizontal divider, held in the frame by a thin rod that runs through holes in the middle of each bead. The bottom 5 beads represented the digits 1 through 5, whereas the two beads in the top half represented units of 5 each. The right-most column represented the 'ones' column; the next one to the left was the 'tens' column; the next one to the left was the 'hundreds' column, etc.

work overalls. These prices might seem low by current standards but most prices were cheaper then as you could go to the movies for 12 cents for children or buy a comic book for 5 cents.

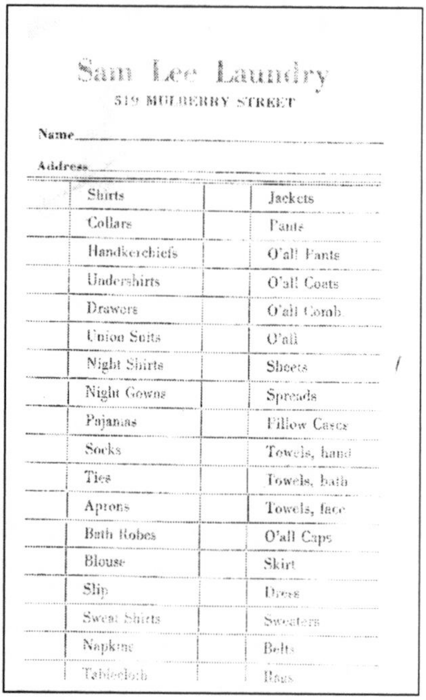

Sam Lee Laundry
519 MULBERRY STREET

Name

Address

Shirts	Jackets
Collars	Pants
Handkerchiefs	O'all Pants
Undershirts	O'all Coats
Drawers	O'all Comb.
Union Suits	O'all
Night Shirts	Sheets
Night Gowns	Spreads
Pajamas	Pillow Cases
Socks	Towels, hand
Ties	Towels, bath
Aprons	Towels, face
Bath Robes	O'all Caps
Blouse	Skirt
Slip	Dress
Sweat Shirts	Sweaters
Napkins	Belts
Tablecloth	Rags

Figure 22 Our laundry checklist inventory.

After the cost for the final item was included, Father would look at the arrangement of the beads on the abacus and translate that information into the amount to charge the customer for his package of laundry.[48] We then placed the wrapped packages on shelves for distribution to customers when they arrived to claim their laundry. The workday started around 5 or 5:30 am and lasted until after dark, at

[48] Some studies show that an abacus compares favorably with an electronic calculator in speed and accuracy. After father retired, he was attracted by hand-held calculators when they became available in the early 1970s. but he found it difficult to learn how to use them. He always used his abacus to double check his electronic calculations for his rental income.

which time my parents would eat dinner before retiring to rest for the following day when the sequence would be repeated, Mondays through Fridays. We did not do any washing or ironing on Saturdays but were nonetheless busy as most customers came to pick up their laundry on that day.

One advantage of operating a laundry was that we always had clean clothes, towels, and sheets for ourselves. Another was that customers often left valuables in their pockets, and sometimes failed to reclaim them. Besides money, customers left wrist and pocket watches, fountain pens, pocketknives, and jewelry in their clothing articles. Unclaimed items accumulated gradually in Mother's storage cabinet where she kept money collected from the business each night. As we got older, realizing that she had these 'treasures', we began to pester her to let us have some of the booty. I must have received four or five watches from a collection that included Bulova, Hamilton, and Elgin makes, all of which I eventually lost or broke, over-winding them or cracking the crystal covers. She also gave me several fancy Eversharp, Waterman, Parker, and Sheaffer fountain pens that used ink to use for schoolwork.

A much too frequent problem arose when customers lost their laundry tickets. Without a ticket, it was extremely time-consuming and difficult to find a customer's laundry. We would have to determine how long ago the laundry was brought in and the number and types of articles they had. Then we had to do a search package-by-package. Each package that seemed like it might be the correct one had to be opened and the wrong ones had to be rewrapped.

Once we succeeded in finding the right package, the customer had to sign on the ticket listing the items to acknowledge they had collected their laundry in case they later found the ticket and thought we still had their laundry. Many of our customers, white as well as black, were illiterate, and could only mark an "X," to sign off that they received their laundry. Although this type of mistake was rare, customers could be quite belligerent when we could not find laundry that they forgot they had already picked up.[49]

Some customers lost their tickets so often that Father realized it was pointless to give them one. Instead Father tagged their laundry using their initials. When they came in, we simply used their initials in place of a ticket. Because of this procedure, there were some customers whose names I never learned, as I only knew them by their initials.

Undoubtedly the lost ticket problem was pervasive at Chinese laundries all over the country and led to the widespread mimicking expression, "no tickee, no washee," directed in ridicule at Chinese laundrymen. But laundrymen were certainly as justified in requiring a ticket before releasing laundry as a parking attendant was in wanting to see a claim check before letting someone drive a car off the lot. The taunt was just a racist mocking of the way the laundrymen spoke English.

---

[49] An account of one early laundryman was that some men would even falsely "...claim parcels, saying they had lost their tickets, and would fight if they did not get what they asked for. Sometimes we were taken before Magistrates and fined for losing shirts that we had never seen." Lee Chew, "The Biography of a Chinaman," *Independent*, 15 (19 February 1903): 417–423.

Sometimes problems would arise with customers angry about real or imagined damage to their articles of clothing. Old clothing might tear or a worker might scorch a sheet. Or, a customer might mistakenly think that some of his laundry was missing. These irate customers would demand payment for replacing these items. Usually, these disagreements were resolved, because Father stood his ground and eventually the customer gave up. Once, however, one customer seriously threatened physical violence. I was very young, probably 5 or 6, and Mother screamed at me to go get help. I vaguely recall dashing for help at Oscar's bar next to the hotel. Luckily, I managed to get someone who came and calmed the irate customer. Running a laundry certainly involved more than just washing and ironing clothes![50]

---

[50] Father retired and sold the Sam Lee Laundry in 1956. When I visited Macon in 1967, the building had been remodeled but was no longer a laundry. On a visit in 2003, I discovered this building that housed a Chinese laundry for about 75 years was now just another parking lot.

5. Family and Social Life

Running a laundry afforded financial independence for my parents but it was extremely demanding, starting before dawn and ending after dark. For them there was nothing else to do in Macon but work. What would my parents have done with leisure time? They neither understood nor enjoyed American culture enough to comprehend or appreciate movies. Television in those days was not available in Macon and even if it had been, the programs would not have meant anything to them. Lacking proficient English speaking, reading, or writing skills, they were unable to socialize with either whites or blacks so that everything, for them, centered on work and family.

Their only window to the outside world was through the Chinese newspaper that came from either San Francisco or New York. The strange-looking characters printed up and down the pages intrigued me. After dinner, they would sometimes discuss news related to either events in China or to issues pertaining to Chinese in America, stimulated by information obtained from the Chinese newspaper. This was the source from which Mother learned news about incidents of atrocities and violence committed against Chinese people across the country, incidents she cited often to warn us about racial prejudice.

There were no Chinese adults who could provide them with information or even opinions about world events. They did not read the local newspaper or listen to the radio for news because they did not understand enough English. Years later, Mother would occasionally reflect that for a while she felt she was going crazy and was afraid she was forgetting how to speak Chinese because there was no one other than her husband she could converse with on adult topics. And, we children were too young to discuss important societal issues or political events with them. They were quite isolated from the larger world.

Aside from what we children learned at school, our window to the world and the larger society was our radio, which sat atop our Servel refrigerator. We kids would listen avidly each week to the classic comedy radio shows such as *Dagwood and Blondie, Our Miss Brooks, My Friend Irma, Jack Benny, Amos and Andy, Fibber McGee and Molly, Edgar Bergen and Charlie McCarthy,* and quiz shows such as *Stop the Music.* We also listened to shows like *Lux Radio Theatre,* and the *Lone Ranger,* but we avoided scary shows like *Inner Sanctum,* with its sinister sounding squeaking door that started each episode, or *Gangbusters,* which opened with screaming police sirens. I also got hooked on the after school radio serialized action dramas aimed at young boys such as *Jack Armstrong, the All-American Boy, Captain Midnight, Superman,* and *Sky King.* Breakfast cereals such as Wheaties, promoted as the Breakfast of Champions, or Kellogg's Pep sponsored most of them, and they cleverly offered items that appealed to young boys such as 'secret decoder rings.' Since you had to send in a cereal box top and a small amount of money, I ended up nagging Mother until she let me buy these products, which she had never purchased before.

Little cockroaches darting across the dial of the radio sometimes enlivened our listening enjoyment. Since the insides of the old vacuum tube radios were hot, roaches liked to seek refuge inside the radio box. Fortunately these were the small ones measuring about the size of the fingernail on your little finger; down in the laundry, there were large ones, about the size of your large toenail that emerged at night.

We would occasionally see little mice scurrying around our living quarters at night. They did not seem too dangerous, but they were unwelcome sights. We would set baited mousetraps and occasionally kill a few of them. But the really scary creatures were the larger gray rats, at least 4 or 5 inches long, especially after both of my sisters had the misfortune of being bitten on their toes while they were asleep at night.

I never knew how or why my parents had a collection of 78-rpm phonograph records of American popular music. In a corner of the front room of our living space, there was a phonograph that you had to crank to supply the energy to play the records. I never saw my parents ever play any records, but I found some of their collection very entertaining. My favorites were *For me and my gal, The Vamp, Begin the Beguine,* and one that I recall even though I don't know the exact title because it had the intriguing lyric, *"Who's that knocking on the hen house door, Henry?"* As the old 78 rpm records were easily broken if you dropped them, we lost a large part of the collection due to our carelessness.

They had only a few Chinese records, but one was the Chinese national anthem.[51] It had a lively martial drumbeat and chant, which we

---

[51] Known as "Chee Lai" or March of the Volunteers, it was sung during the resistance against the Japanese in China and later it became the national anthem of the People's Republic of China.

enjoyed immensely. George, Jean, and I would march around our parents' bed to the rhythm of this anthem, which we dubbed the "dum dum" song after the sound of a drum roll at the start of the anthem leading into the chorus.

A favorite evening pastime for us kids after we closed the laundry was to stroll around town to view store window displays. Father would sometimes accompany us on these window-shopping walks, but Mother never did, possibly because she was tired after cooking dinner and washing the dishes. Our favorite stores were those with displays of watches, jewelry, shoes, clothing, luggage, and furniture that we sometimes wished we had.

Sometimes we would 'splurge' and use the weighing machines in front of some stores. You would insert a penny and the machine would dispense a small cardboard, about 1x2 inches, with your weight printed it on one side and a picture of a movie star on the other side. The excitement was to see if your card had a star you liked since we more or less knew our weight already. With a bit more money we might buy a 5-cent cup of ice cream that similarly had a picture of a movie star inside. To see it, you just licked the ice cream off the inside of the cup lid.

One disturbing aspect of these walks was seeing disabled people, mostly blind people and amputees, sitting on the sidewalk in front of stores. Some played harmonicas and others had a display of pencils, hoping that passersby would donate money. It was not the 'begging' that bothered me as much as discovering the existence of people afflicted with such severe physical limitations. It was upsetting but it also made me appreciate being able-bodied.

During the hot summer evenings after our walks around town, or even on nights when we were too tired to take our strolls, we dragged chairs out of the store to sit on in front of the laundry to cool off before going to bed. And, although it was still rather warm from baking in the Georgia sun all day, we used, as a bench, the base for a barrier that was embedded in the sidewalk to prevent pedestrians from accidentally falling onto a set of stairs that led to a basement store next to our front door to our living quarters.

Figure 23 Mary and Jean on the 'bench' anchoring our 'jungle gym.'

As part of this barrier, a fence made from galvanized pipes with two horizontal bars about 2' apart rose about 4' above the granite base it was mounted in. These pipes provided George and me with convenient play apparatus to climb on.

Sunday was the day of rest. In a small, sleepy town, there was not much for our family to do but relax. After rising late, Father did routine maintenance as well as occasional repairs on equipment while Mother prepared meals. Otherwise, the day was used to recover from the past week of hard work and to prepare for the next week. Our laundry, like all other commercial businesses in those days, except for movie theaters and soda fountains was closed. Even then, sometimes customers who forgot to claim their laundry on Saturday took advantage of the fact that we lived above the laundry. They would awaken us early Sunday, banging on our door and demanding that we let them get their laundry. Among the worst offenders were some of the bellboys from the Lanier Hotel.

The routine of small town life was broken by two special events that came to town once each year, the county fair and the circus. These events were really exciting for us children. The fair was held outdoors during the summer, which could be very uncomfortable in the daytime, so we waited until evening when the temperature was cooler. We liked to watch people on the amusement rides like the ferris wheel and thrill rides especially when they screamed, but I was too timid to go on most of them. We played games of chance, and strolled along the midway to listen with a mixture of wonder, skepticism, and sometimes, disgust at the barkers hawking their freak shows. Of course, we looked at all the prize livestock on display although the smells were not that enjoyable. Father would take us when we were very young, but Mother never came along. The

Ringling Brothers circus was even more exciting. Their shows were performed in the city auditorium just a few blocks from our laundry. Like all kids, I was enthralled by the acrobatic acts, the lion tamers, the elephants, and of course, the clowns.

We never took vacations because operating a family laundry required a six-day week for all 52 weeks each year. When students returned to school each September and boasted about their wonderful summer family vacations, the concept was foreign to my experience. I had just assumed everyone stayed home from school during the summer break like we did. Before I attended school, I had no idea that families took long trips away from home. Never having been on a vacation in my life, I did not 'miss' them, but I was a bit envious.

Mother and Father's Relationship

Traditionally in China, women hold inferior status to men. Sons were valued as sources of labor and income as well as progenitors of the family lineage. Daughters, on the other hand were viewed as liabilities; they had to be fed, and produced little or no income. In addition, upon marriage, they had to transfer their allegiance to the husband's family. It was rumored that in difficult times baby girls were drowned to avoid expenses. In the intensely patriarchal Chinese society it is hardly surprising that Chinese marriages are male dominated and that wives have little voice in marital decisions. Unlike the Western belief in romantic love as the basis for marriage, economic necessity and raising a family were decisive. A successful match was fortunate.An incompatible match was unfortunate, but the couple had little recourse and no alternatives, as divorce was unavailable. Growing up in America, we children embraced the notion that marriage was based on romance and love. Yet, at the same time we saw that this concept did not apply to our parents. We were shocked and dismayed when we learned that in China arranged marriages had been the tradition for centuries.

On the surface, our parents' marriage seemed harmonious. But it was difficult for us to accurately judge the quality of their marriage because the only criteria we knew were the romantic portrayals we saw in the movies. Mother often complained bitterly to us that Father made her do all the hard work while he had it easy. On numerous occasions, she would cite the difficult early years when she had to get up before dawn to take my sisters with her and a black worker, as well as laundry packages, to the pickup and dropout office several blocks away while Father got to sleep longer before opening the main store.

Figure 24 Mary and her nanny at the Great Southern Laundry office on Cotton Ave.

She would also relate that she would have never managed alone. Usually one of the black women who worked in the laundry helped her with the trek between the two stores, acting as nanny for the girls and as her teacher of English language and American customs.

Whenever Mother and Father argued, there was no one who could mediate or attempt to reconcile conflicts. Language, as well as cultural barriers, made that impossible. Neither had another adult with whom they could speak to in their native language, even if they had been willing to do so. Perhaps complaining to her children became a way to let Mother ventilate her frustrations. Even though we could not fully comprehend the real issues we understood enough Chinese to know what she was complaining about. But we were only young children and we could not give her advice for resolving any conflicts.

I never witnessed any physical aggression on Father's part but on one unforgettable occasion I saw Mother was very distraught. She had packed some belongings in a suitcase, and she was crying as she struggled carrying it down Mulberry Street toward the train station about four blocks away. Her intention was to go to Atlanta to seek refuge with Father's brother. It was an act of desperation, as she did not know any other Chinese person within 100 miles that she could turn to for comfort or assistance. I was too young to know exactly what had happened to provoke her actions, but I was frightened when I saw her leaving. Jean recalls noticing that she had a black eye so Father must have been physically abusive. I do not recall how the crisis was resolved but some customers or neighboring merchants probably interceded and persuaded her not to leave.

More commonly they shouted and criticized each other. Mother's worst "curse" was to tell him "to go and die." He was verbally less extreme, disparaging her views or telling her she was talking nonsense.

A continuing bone of contention between them was that Father regularly sent money back to his family in China. He also helped his younger brother financially to come to the U. S. in 1936. Mother resented it because he did not allow her to send money to her family. And while I can saw her point from an American perspective, I wonder if her indignation was warranted from a Chinese perspective that held that when a daughter married, her allegiance was to the husband's family.

By American criteria, their marriage was probably not a 'happy' one, but by Chinese standards, it might be said that it was somewhat typical, if not always tolerable. I never suspected any major problems existed in the marriage when I was a child, although I know Mother often 'nagged' or ridiculed Father for his behavior, sometimes in front of him and sometimes just to us children. Father usually ignored her complaints. He was generally relaxed and slow to anger. Occasionally, she would remind us about some of Father's decisions that did not work out well. Or she might cite instances when he had been ill, which she attributed to his poor eating habits or excessive smoking, a habit he indulged in whenever he took a work break.

Mother was probably venting her frustration much of the time, although I realized later that she had some valid complaints about the quality of her marital relationship. As a child, however, it was difficult for me to conclude that Father was as 'inept' as Mother often depicted him. In fact, her scolding of Father probably made me feel more sympathetic toward him. It was not that I was unsympathetic to her distress, but I sometimes felt she was overdoing it. I came to discount her ranting because I heard them so often and because they seemed to place her as superior to Father who was depicted as selfish or thoughtless.

My Relationship with Father

These reactions to conflicts between my parents could have been biased because I felt I had a generally good relationship with Father. He was proud of my academic success, and usually allowed me to pursue my own interests. His only requirements for me were that I help out in the laundry, often at times when I preferred to be playing. Growing up, I felt closest to him on our occasional trips to visit his brother and other Chinese laundrymen in Atlanta. Otherwise, he had no time to spend with me as he worked long hours doing hard physical work. In his little free time, he would read his Chinese newspaper from San Francisco. As I grew up, I grew away from him, as we did not have much in common. This should not be a surprise, as the expected father-son relationship differs for Chinese and Americans. Chinese favor a more formal and distant relationship, whereas Americans strive for a warmer, almost buddy-like, father-son connection.

One hot, muggy summer night when I was about 8, he and I had taken a stroll downtown to cool off after the laundry closed. We stopped to rest on a park bench across from the Bibb Theater, which often showed cowboy movies. For reasons I will never know, he decided to take me into the theater where we saw a Grade B western starring Tex Ritter. The plot followed the usual good guys in the white hats and bad guys in the black hats scenario. I wonder now if Father appreciated or even understood the movie. For me it was a magical experience, and I quickly became a regular at the other theater that featured westerns, the Ritz. Every Saturday matinee the theater showed a double feature, two westerns starring favorites like Hopalong Cassidy, Lash LaRue, Red Ryder, or the Rough Riders. Along with the featured westerns, they showed serialized action thrillers such as "Dick Tracy." At the end of each of 15 weekly episodes, except the final one, the hero had apparently met his doom, either falling over a cliff in a burning car or trapped inside a burning building on the top floor. We eagerly returned every week to find out how our hero survived the latest obstacle, as he always did. A *Three Stooges* slapstick comedy episode was usually also included in the program, which lasted for about 3 hours.

Often on Saturdays when work was busy at the laundry, I might have to wait until later in the day to get to the movies or sometimes even missed an entire show, but George always found a way to sneak off to the cowboy movies. Occasionally I was dispatched to search for George and to summon him home to help out in the laundry, so he soon learned to duck down behind seats when he spotted me in the theater looking for him.

We also went to see the more commercially successful films of Roy Rogers, one of the 'singing cowboys,' which were never shown at the Ritz, which played only grade B movies. The better movies, including dramas and musicals, played at the Capitol. Roy Rogers's movies were filmed in Technicolor, whereas all the B-westerns were in black and white. Roy Rogers' films were different from the other cowboy films because they had a plot that involved more than just heading the bank robbers or rustlers off at the pass. Roy had a beautiful palomino horse, Trigger, who was classier than the average cowboy's horse. Moreover, Roy was not your strictly macho cowboy. Although he did engage in fisticuffs with the bad guys, he also had a girlfriend, Dale Evans. However, there was no kissing or overt romance. And at some point in every movie, he would also break out into singing while strumming a guitar and accompanied by a cowhand chorus, the Sons of the Pioneers.

Father was fairly generous whenever I wanted some spending money to buy toys or go to the movies. If he was in the proper mood, I could get him to let us buy ice cream cones or the Sunday newspaper. But the most memorable expenditure that Father made for me came one day when a World Book Encyclopedia salesman appeared at the laundry. He showed us samples of the contents, with colored maps and many other illustrations. I was enthralled by the detailed information about interesting topics as well as by the beautiful bright red covers. Father saw how excited I was and asked me if I would find the encyclopedia helpful for school. Unable to contain my enthusiasm, I was probably speechless but I didn't need to say anything. Without hesitation, Father purchased a set. I don't know how much it cost, but I am certain it was not an inexpensive purchase for a family in our position. When the more than 20 volumes finally arrived in several installments over several weeks, I spent many happy and enlightening hours browsing through them.

As we children grew older, it became our task to read and explain financial and legal documents that Father would receive but not be able to read or understand. Inasmuch as our proficiency in Chinese was not very great, it was often impossible for us to translate adequately for our parents. In 1946 Father decided to become a naturalized citizen, which meant he had to learn some basic information about our governmental system, laws, and history. Now I became his teacher, as he needed me to translate words, explain historical facts, or interpret political terms while he prepared for his exam, which turned out to be very easy. So, in 1948 he became a U. S. citizen.

Overall, my relationship with Father, though formal, was positive. He was a generally a calm, soft-spoken person, quite the opposite of Mother who was more outspoken and opinionated, and quick to offer advice on virtually any topic.

My Relationship with George

As the older brother, it was natural that I would try to control the play with George. Moreover, as George was developmentally disabled, my dominance was even greater. When we were very young, we did not own many toys purchased from stores so we had to improvise. Once I devised a game in which we each held one of Mother's small makeup mirrors, and while lying on our backs on our parents' bed, we played a form of 'sunray tag.' The goal was to first catch the sun's light on your mirror, redirect it onto the ceiling, and try to keep your reflected light away from your brother's reflected light.

Another game involved empty soft drink bottles and unopened tin cans of food. We would stack them like building blocks or play war using them as soldiers. Once we were old enough to play checkers, we would use bottle caps from soft drinks in place of red and black checker pieces, playing games between Coca Cola and Pepsi, or R. C. Cola and Nehi Orange, for example. When we got older, our games were more physically active and we enjoyed playing cops and robbers, hide and seek, or chase. And of course, once I had developed my passion for cowboy movies, we played roles as lawmen and outlaws. We each had toy cap pistols to serve as our six shooters. Depending on my current hero, I either had two matching pistols and holsters like Red Ryder or Roy Rogers or managed with a single pistol like the Durango Kid. Our horses were imaginary but we ran in a gallop, and made clippity-clop sounds with our mouths to add realism.

George and I spent a lot of time playing with our red Radio Flyer wagon. We took turns pushing each other in the wagon, speeding down Mulberry Street as fast as we could. We roared full speed past the Lanier Hotel and coasted past the laundry until we came to a gradual stop as we reached the corner filling station. Fortunately, the sidewalk was very wide, and we managed to steer clear of pedestrians.

When George and I were about 6 or 7, Father assigned us the Sunday morning responsibility of dusting the shelves where the wrapped packages of finished laundry were stacked. We also had to move all of the yet unclaimed packages up to the front of the store.

Figure 25   Giving George a piggyback ride in front of our laundry c. 1950

These two rows of shelves, about 6' across, were suspended from the ceiling to a level that an adult could reach to place or retrieve packages. Starting from just behind the front counter where customers waited to be served, the shelves extended into the store about 15 feet, to the area where Father wrapped each customer's laundry in brown paper.

To do our dusting chores, George and I would scamper up over the sorting table that was used during workdays to assemble the laundry items for each customer. We had to climb above it to get into the shelf area.   We made the chore into a game, especially in the summer, turning on the two large fans that hung from the ceiling above the front counter and pretending we were flying a B-29 on bombing missions over Japan in World War II. Usually I was the pilot, and George, the co-pilot. Sometimes we let one-person pilot while the other crawled to the back of the shelf assembly, to serve as the bombardier or rear gunner. We ignored the fact that the engines of the plane, the electric fans, were actually not connected to our 'plane' but were about six feet to the front of the shelving. Of course, unlike the engines on a real plane, our make-believe ones faced *toward* us but that was a minor concern to us, as we preferred to be cooled by the fans blowing into our faces rather than have the more realistic arrangement of fans blowing air away from us. All the while engaged in our fantasies, we managed to take the feather dusters and clean the shelves, and to find time to move unclaimed laundry packages scattered across the shelves to the front so that there would be room for next week's packages.

I would sometimes coax George to play baseball or basketball with me. Even though he was not that well coordinated, George would play until he got bored. He threw the ball, and I, with my oversized Ted Williams autographed Louisville slugger bat tried to hit it. We were pretty terrible, which was just as well given that we played in the sand lot behind the Christ Church parish house, which had many small windowpanes that were at our mercy. Unable to avoid breaking a few of them, we had to face the church staff more than once. They were forgiving, but convinced us to use a big 12-inch diameter rubber ball instead of a baseball.

When he was old enough attend school, George's learning difficulties created problems. A slow learner and inattentive, George would often be sent to the principal's office or home. Special education was not yet widely available. The school system was not prepared or able to offer help, and none of the family really knew what could be done to improve his schooling. School was very frustrating for

George, and he soon learned to be a truant.

Mother, unable to understand his problem, of course, was very protective of George. He was allowed to do as he pleased. As his older brother, I tried to 'motivate' him, but being immature myself, I really did not know how to deal with him either, often wrongly berating or scolding him.

George found an escape at the movies. Radio programs were not as engaging for George as for Jean or me. He preferred going to see an afternoon fare of cowboy movies, "Three Stooges" episodes, and a Superman or Dick Tracy serial. For some unknown reason, George referred to the movies as "baby shows" and he would tear out movie ads from the newspaper and play with them as if they were treasured toys just as I might play with toy cars or Jean with her dolls.

The small-town atmosphere of Macon cushioned George's problems, especially since he was still a child. He was happy, despite his lack of success in school. It is difficult to know how racial matters affected him. Clearly he knew that our family, himself included, was Chinese and different from everyone else in town who was either black or white. But how important that was to him or whether he ever felt racial discrimination is hard to say.

My Sisters

As Mary was six years older, I do not have many vivid memories of her because we probably did not spend much time together as children. She spent her free time with her girlfriends at their houses but she did occasionally help at the front counter to wait on customers. As the eldest child, Mary also had to be the 'interpreter' of documents written in English that our parents could not read.

When we were very young, she had the responsibility of looking after George and me when we were outside playing. Sometimes she or Jean, or both of them, would engage us in hopscotch, ring around the rosies, and other simple children's games. I was 12 when Mary moved to San Francisco. The fact that I hardly recall missing her suggests that we did not do many things together as kids. However, once the rest of us moved to San Francisco, we had a much stronger relationship.

I spent more time with Jean, but even she was three years older than me, and we had separate interests. We did spend time reading comic books together, especially *Wonder Woman* and *Looney Toons*, and when we were older, there was a period when we tried to educate each other by reading aloud such books as *Jane Eyre* and Poe's *Gold Bug*.

As we got older I spent less time with my sisters because I was more interested in athletic activities while they were more involved in activities such as playing with dolls or giving each other Toni home permanents. Both of my sisters had more social contact with their classmates than I did with mine. They would go to birthday parties and participate in other social activities with their girlfriends.

What Mother Taught Us about Health

I never heard either of my parents speak specifically of the Chinese views of yin and yang balance, but they did adhere to the Chinese explanatory concepts of illnesses being related to weak constitution, excess wind (feng) or cool temperature (*leung*). We were cautioned against eating too much fried food (*geet hay*). We were not allowed to drink ice water with meals. They believed that remedies involved restoring balance, by offsetting the condition at fault. I was always dubious, because it seemed too simplistic to dichotomize foods into either hot or cold categories.

According to Mother, Father's general health was a continual problem. She claimed he had a weak constitution all of his life so he always needed lots of rest and sleep. Still, like Mother, he managed to work everyday, week in and week out, year after year. Being sick was no excuse not to work for either of them, because the work would not do itself. He did take up cigarette smoking, usually when taking a work break. Mother criticized him frequently for this behavior, and she warned us not to follow his example. Fortunately, he quit smoking shortly before he retired. Father did not really drink liquor very much, although he did occasionally have a shot of bourbon at dinner or a few swallows of a Chinese rice wine, *ng ka pay,* but I never saw him intoxicated.

Eventually he suffered from high blood pressure. We were worried when we noticed swollen bumps in the veins along his forearms when he was in his forties. We did not see them, but he may have had them on his legs. They may have been varicose veins, as laundrymen had to spend many hours each day on their feet. I don't know what medical treatment he received, but fortunately these bumps did eventually go away.

During her early years in Georgia during her childbearing period, Mother often experienced fatigue from malnutrition and lack of adequate food. Mother also suffered relatively minor health problems related to asthma and hay fever. The pollens of spring and the heat and humidity of summer, which made life very uncomfortable, exacerbated these ailments. She often would later describe occasions when she was so sick she could hardly work. On at least one occasion, surgery for her ailments was recommended, advice that she adamantly declined and lived to talk about. She proudly talked about how doctors were not as successful as she was in treating her ailments. She boasted that she always tried one folk remedy after another until something worked. She had a strong distrust of doctors, and felt that home remedies were more effective. In general, even on issues other than health, her conviction was that she could solve most problems through sheer fortitude and determination. Whenever we would get sick or have a health problem, she would often give us folk remedies and Chinese herbs purchased from San Francisco. She would warn us against accepting every recommendation or treatment from American doctors. It is fortunate that Mother was able to successfully deal with her health problems as well as she did because HMOs or medical and health insurance were not then available to us. Whenever any of us had to see a doctor or a dentist or buy medicines, we had to bear the entire cost.

What Our Parents Taught Us about Religion

Neither Mother nor Father practiced or preached any type of formal religion, Western or Eastern. They never tried to teach us anything about religion except indirectly. Mother's basic message was that most religious people were hypocrites. That is not exactly her wording; she would point out that some people who go to church one day would kill or rob on the next day. Since our parents did not adhere to any religious practices it is no surprise that we would not attend church either.

However, some of our well-intentioned white customers were concerned about our fate. They seemed to assume we were heathens, atheists, or maybe Buddhists, but that in any case, they needed to save us with Christianity. Dr. William Burke, the same Methodist missionary who a generation earlier brought the three Soong sisters[52] to attend college in Macon, persuaded my parents to allow him to take my sisters to Sunday school each week. I was never included, perhaps because I was too young. They often came home singing, "Jesus loves me, this I know, The Bible tells me so," but I did not have a clue what any of it meant at that age.

One day one of our customers, obviously of a Christian persuasion and with a missionary zeal, came into the laundry and presented my parents with two 8x10 framed pictures, one of the nativity and one of the crucifixion. Apparently, they felt that we heathens needed to have a Christian religious influence in our home.

Not knowing anything about the significance of the themes, I proudly hung them on the wall near my parents' bed. They were probably the only pictures we ever had, aside from two family portraits,

---

[52]Daughters of a Chinese who made a fortune selling Bibles in China became the most powerful women in China. The eldest, Ai-Ling, married the future finance minister, H. H. Kung, the second eldest, Ching-Ling, married Sun Yat Sen, leader of the 1911 revolution that lead to the formation of the Chinese republic, and the youngest, Mei-Ling, married Chiang Kai-Shek, leader of the Nationalist government.

which sat on Mother's dressing table. None of our walls bore any other decorative art. The nativity scene was tranquil, and I readily enjoyed looking at it. But my attention was more strongly directed to the crucifixion picture. I was more curious and perplexed than frightened by the sight of Jesus on the cross, naked except for a cloth covering his loins, with nails in his hands and feet, and blood dripping out from them. Neither of these pictures seemed to faze either of my parents who seemed to just ignore them.

I can recall hearing the church bells toll on Sunday mornings, as the Christ Church was on the opposite side of the same block as our laundry. One Sunday morning, I asked Father about the bells. Who was ringing them and why? After he told me that the bells were announcing the beginning of church services, I asked why we did not go to church. His explanation was that *lo fan*, or *wai goey* (white ghosts) as white people were also referred to, were evil and sinful during the week and they needed to go to church to atone on Sunday. By implication, *baak goey* (black ghosts) or black people needed church for much the same reasons. However, we Chinese[53] were good during the week, so he argued, and thus we had no need to go to church on Sunday.

This answer was reassuring; at least when I was very young and I did not question it. Our parents did not attend church and they did

---

[53]Interestingly, there was no term for yellow ghosts, as Chinese were simply, 'yellow people.' As a child I never realized this imbalance in terms for different races. Later I understood that by speaking of whites and blacks as 'ghosts' the Chinese meant to derogate them; hence, there was no counterpart of 'yellow ghosts' to use for speaking about people of our own race.

not encourage or expect us to go either. Still, I felt like we were missing out on something by not going to church. None of us attended any religious services of any type in Macon.

What Our Parents Taught Us about Money

As we were growing up, Mother continually would 'lecture' us about the importance of thrift and economy. Waste was abhorrent to her and we all learned the necessity of saving all types of resources. She 'recycled' long before it became fashionable, as she never discarded anything that could be reused such as string, paper clips, rubber bands, and paper napkins. In buying food and clothing, she always looked for bargains or bottom-of-the-line quality.

Combining their hard work and light spending, over the years they accumulated more money than might appear possible. Some of these funds were sent to help Father's family in China over the years. These resources would provide the foundation for our family's move to San Francisco and enable my parents to purchase real estate there.

Our parents always paid cash for anything they bought, no matter how much it cost. They never bought anything on layaway or credit. They simply never went into debt; if they did not have enough money, they just waited until they saved it. Rarely did they even use checks, except to pay utility bills, preferring to deal in cold cash. I guess this was not unique to my parents, as even now I notice many Asian immigrants carry rather sizeable wads of paper money to pay for purchases rather than rely on credit cards.

Whether it was because they were immigrants who were anxious about their future or because of their harrowing experience of the Great Depression of the 1930s, my parents not only were very frugal but they also hoarded their financial assets. Considerable sums of cash, in the form of $20 and higher denomination bills were hidden in empty half-gallon Karo syrup cans.

When I was no older than 8 and 9, Father took me into his confidence by telling me about this cache of money. He took me to the foot of the back stairs leading into the laundry. There he pried loose several of the steps to show me where he had hidden several Karo cans filled with money in the empty space beneath these steps. This treasure was to be kept secret and I was to retrieve the money in the event that something "bad" happened to our parents.

Similarly, Mother entrusted me, as the oldest son, with her secret supply of money. Her method was to stuff paper bills in an emptied talcum powder tin container and to replace some talcum powder to cover the wad of money. These caches were hidden around the house. I suspect that she never let Father know about this money, as she was saving it for her own family in China eventually. It was both exciting and frightening for me to know about these hidden treasuries. There was pride in being trusted but also anxiety over the burden of these responsibilities.

We didn't get a weekly 'allowance' of spending money. Whenever we wanted money to spend on toys and candy, we would petition, plead, or beg our parents. Overall, they were reasonable and although they sometimes declined our requests, they usually gave us small amounts from time to time for our personal use.

Still I wanted to earn my own money so when I was about 8, I decided to sell newspapers. A classmate, Tootsie Williams, had a paper route that I helped him with occasionally. I soon wanted my own route but I didn't have a bicycle, so I went to the newspaper office every afternoon and they would give me a supply of newspapers that I would try to sell on street corners, with the proviso that I could return any unsold copies to the office. I don't recall what my percent of the take was, but I didn't do well and soon gave up.

I finally convinced Mother to let me buy a bicycle when I was about 10, thinking I could then get my own paper route. I paid about $40 for a shiny new red and white bicycle but had to walk it home several blocks from the Western Auto store because I didn't yet know how to ride a bike. Jean also was a novice, so we took turns encouraging each other. We kept crashing my shiny new bike into walls and falling onto the ground trying to learn how to ride in the yard between the back of our laundry and the Christ Church parish house. By the time I learned to ride, I lost interest in having a paper route.

One other money making venture involved my dismal attempt to sell packets of flower and vegetable seeds. Comic books sometimes ran enticing ads on the back cover to convince gullible kids how easy it was to make money selling seeds so I sent off for a supply. I was a total failure, as even my own mother would not buy any seeds, and I had to send back most of them unsold except for the few I bought myself to save face.

Some of Mother's Misconceptions and Quirks

Despite her limited contact with American culture and the English language, Mother generally managed to learn American customs and values simply by observation. However, a few of her ideas were totally wrong. For example, back in the late 1940s street photographers would take candid shots of people as they walked on city streets. They would then give you a card with an address where you could view and purchase copies of these candid shots. Mother thought that the photographers wanted your picture to sell to others so she would warn us to avoid having photographs taken of us, and to avert our gaze from any cameras pointed at us.

During the opening frames of some newsreels shown at movie theatres, the audience sees a movie camera aimed at a news scene. Suddenly, it turns 180 degrees so that it is then aimed directly at the theatre audience. Mother believed this camera took images of audience members for sale to the movie studios. She warned us to look away or cover our faces whenever the camera was pointed at us. I never recalled her ever attending a movie, but obviously she must have gone at least once to even know these newsreels existed. But why, with her limited knowledge of English, she would have gone to a movie is beyond my understanding.

These misconceptions fit a worldview couched in suspicion and distrust, hardly surprising for her since this outlook was protective against possible harm in a segregationist era. Of course, there were other instances where it is less certain as to whether her conclusions that racism was involved were valid. She generally felt all government agencies were biased against Chinese. She would cite the example of the competing dry cleaners next door operated by a white person who succeeded in getting the city to allow a yellow zone in front of his store for his customers to park momentarily to pick up and drop off clothing. But Father was denied the same type of petition on the grounds that there would be too many yellow zones if he were also to receive one.

Mother was also very concerned that when we grew up we might marry someone who was not Chinese. Given that we were the only Chinese in Macon, if we stayed there, her concerns were well founded. Additionally, as did many other states, Georgia had strong laws against miscegenation, but she probably did not know that. She simply believed that marriages of *lo fan*, or white people, were highly likely to end in divorce.

As cautionary tales, she would often relate accounts of some Chinese men who had married white women, but had later been deserted or divorced by them. It was not so much that she was prejudiced against whites, but felt that if we married whites, we and our children would never be fully accepted by most whites. I 'rebelled' mildly at her generalizations about mixed marriages and would often tease her that I was going to marry a 'green' person when I grew up.

Mother gave us life lessons on less serious issues as well. Being cautious, she was always a careful observer of people. Thus, she noticed that whenever the owner of the Lanier Hotel, Mr. Hooks, offered us children chewing gum, he gave only half a stick to each of us. Mother used his frugality as a life lesson, pointing out that even a wealthy man like Mr. Hooks was thrifty and that had he given us each a full stick, he certainly would not be as rich.

Mother's practical nature often dictated her advice. In selecting clothing, for example, she taught us to always consider how well a garment's color could hide dirt. Not surprisingly, most of our wardrobe consisted of dark colors. At the grocery store, she craftily warned us to avoid taking perishable foods from the front of the display, suspicious that they were not as fresh as items placed further back.

I came to discount many of Mother's views and wrote them off to her lack of education and superstitions. My reasoning was that if she could seriously think that the film on the screen in the theater could capture images of people in the audience, then surely she could not be that accurate in her other views. I felt that her limited education was responsible for the way she thought on these matters so I did not argue with her when I disagreed with her views.

Social Contacts

When I started school, I became friends with Richard, a Jewish classmate. After school, I would sometimes walk with him to his house, only a block from the school, on my way back to the laundry three blocks further down the street. Sometimes he would invite me into his family residence. I never had a chance to enter the home of any other child because most of the students did not live in the downtown section.

In fact, Richard almost insisted that I spend time after school in his home, as he was an only child and his parents were both at work. In his parents' apartment, his nanny, a middle-aged black woman who also did cleaning and prepared meals for their family, would supervise us. Richard had the nicest toys, and we got to play with his expensive

Lionel electric train set or erector set, items that I could not even dream of owning. Richard also had spending money, and he often would buy the kind of items from the local games and novelty store, Trick Shop, that fascinated young kids. He had a pair of Scottie dog figures, one black and one white plastic Scottish terrier dog, each about the size of your thumbnail that enthralled me. The fascination stemmed from the small magnet glued underneath each dog. When you moved one dog near the other one, if the poles of the magnets facing each other were of the same polarity, one dog would repel the other dog. If the poles facing each other were opposed in polarity, the dogs would be drawn toward each other. I had never known about magnets, so the effect was magical.

Once in a while, if one of his parents came home while I was there, they would offer to drive me home. Even though the ride only lasted three blocks, it was exciting not only because they had a nice car, but because it was one of the few times I ever rode in an automobile. My parents did not know how to drive, and even if they did, there really was no place for us to go in it. We lived where we worked. We did not know anyone who would invite us for social visits in their homes. And, we had no time to take vacations. A car would have been useless for us.

My other early playmate was a black boy, M. C., about a year older than I. His mother worked for Mr. Harry Spivey, a Negro who had operated a tailor shop since the late 1930s above the store next door. M. C. came after school and waited for her to finish work. We would sometimes sit on our front stairs and read comics. M. C. learned a few phrases of Chinese from hanging out with me. One day, when we were eating lunch inside, we heard someone yell in Chinese, "open the door." Since Mother always barricaded the front door with an iron crossbar, we always had to call her, in Chinese, to open the door whenever we wanted to come in. As all of us were already inside, we had a big laugh because we realized that it had to be M. C. parroting our Chinese password.

M. C. and I would often go to the church parking lot to play basketball. One day Father told me that a customer had seen M. C. and me playing together, and had advised him to teach me not to play with M. C. I was infuriated when Father told me about this warning, but I continued to play with M. C. Father never bothered to say anything more about the issue with me.

A few years later, George and I became friends with Felton, a boy of about my age whose mother operated a boarding house on Walnut Street next door to the church. He was the only child we knew we lived on our block. We did not go to the same school, so I do not know how we met, other than that we lived near each other.

My only other playmate, Jimmy, was a couple of years younger than I. His mother worked for the welfare office that was located next to the south side of the church parish house. Jimmy and his mother lived some distance away, so he would come by after school in the afternoon to wait for his mother to finish work. Felton, Jimmy, George, and I usually played games involving outlaws versus sheriffs. We probably made George play an outlaw more often than not. So, I had this small assortment of very diverse set of playmates as a child.

As for my parents and their social relationships, there were many customers as well as non-customers who, while friendly toward Father and Mother, were not exactly "friends." On the street or in the laundry, they would smile and greet Father, "Hi Sam," because most people naturally assumed from the name of the laundry, that his name was Sam Lee, which it was not. People who were better acquainted with our family knew his real name was Frank Jung. They might comment on the weather or talk about how fast we children were growing. Once in a long while someone might inquire about some aspect of Chinese customs. They sometimes engaged him in conversation about current world or national events, but it is almost certain that Father would have been careful not to offend or express his true feelings on controversial topics. They never invited my parents to their homes to socialize, and that is quite understandable, because they would have had few, if any, common interests.

Mr. Hooks, who owned the Lanier Hotel up the street, was considerate and benevolent to our family even though he was not a customer. Sometimes when he headed out to his nearby farm, he would ask our parents to let us go there with him for the afternoon. It was one of the few times we ever rode in a car, and the only time we went to the countryside. We got to play in a barn with a hayloft, and watch the farm animals get fed. At Christmas, Mr. Hooks always sent us a food basket, mostly containing fruits, as a gift.

Mr. L. A. Shirley was not a customer either. He managed an office building that housed the Grand Theater one block away, and frequently walked past our laundry on his way to and from the Post

Office. Somehow he became friendly with Father and he was very nice and respectful to us children. His office happened to be adjacent to that of our dentist. This is just a conjecture, but probably one day when I was at the dentist, he may have seen me and invited me into his office to chat. In any event, before long, I was making social visits to his office periodically in the late afternoon when his workload was light. He took a special interest in seeing my report card, which was always full of high grades. My guess is that because he had no children, he had more interest in my achievements. He was like a father figure[54] for me and my visits were mutually rewarding.

Figure 26 Mr. Shirley, a family friend who managed the Grand Theater office building.

---

[54] In 1952 after all of us except Father moved from Macon to San Francisco he wrote, in one of many letters, "I pass the store and expect to see some of you--and then it dawns on me that you are 3000 miles away...and I am short five of my very best friends...Don't worry about Dad--or anything back here. We are all o.k. and the old town is running on an even keel."

Mr. Shirley was what you might call a 'Southern gentleman.' He would politely tip his hat to people he knew when he greeted them passing down the street. He would tell me stories of his own boyhood growing up in Vicksburg, Mississippi. Over time, he became a trusted friend of the family, and even served as a witness for Father when became a naturalized citizen in 1948.

Another non-customer who befriended us was an elderly man, Jesse Cooner. He was the clerk in the previously mentioned liquor store next to our laundry. Mr. Cooner was the closest thing to a grandfather for me, as I never got to meet my grandparents in China.

Crammed in a tiny enclosure about 8 feet wide and at most 15 feet deep, Mr. Cooner was surrounded by shelves full of whiskey bottles. As a minor, I broke the law by spending many hours in the liquor store gabbing with Mr. Cooner about one thing or another. An unintended outcome of hanging around there is that I learned the names, prices, and shelf locations of every liquor brand he sold.

On hot summer evenings, Mr. Cooner and I would each pull a chair out of our stores to sit in front out on the sidewalk to cool off. We both enjoyed sitting and discussing the exploits of local and major league baseball teams. Mr. Cooner grew up in the South, so I learned a little about hunting and fishing from him, even though I never actually participated in these activities.

At some point our mutual avid interest in baseball led to our going to Sunday afternoon baseball games at the Luther Williams baseball park, home of our Class A league team, the Macon Peaches, so-called because the region was noted for its peaches. Using his umbrella for shade from the midday sun, we would sit in the top row of the bleachers and root for the home team against other teams from the South Atlantic or 'Sally League.'

Figure 27   Mr. Cooner in his hole-in-the-wall liquor store next door.

During the summer, I would spend a lot of time in his little liquor store discussing major league baseball pennant chases. We would often listen to the radio Game of the Day, which came on most afternoons. We didn't know it at the time, but the announcers were just reconstructing the game from the wire services and not actually in attendance at the ball games they were describing. It was realistic enough for us and we enjoyed them. Mr. Cooner would tease me about my favorite team, the St. Louis Cardinals and my hero, Stan

Musial, when they were not winning many games.

Our Relationship with Teachers

Our teachers at Whittle School knew all of us children well, but I doubt that any of them knew or even met my parents. Not knowing English or having the time, neither Mother nor Father ever attended any school function or PTA meeting. We were a bit embarrassed that our parents did not get involved in any school activities but we realized that they did not understand their purpose. But they dutifully supported requests for money whenever the school asked us to donate materials and money for projects such as sending toothbrushes to soldiers during the war.

Our teachers were strong influences on our development, treating us with respect and helping us to develop self-confidence. My junior high science teacher, Mr. Carr, was my hero. After we moved from Macon, we exchanged letters for over a year about my education. He not only offered encouragement but asked me for advice about how to improve his teaching.[55]

We got along well with other students in and out of class. Most classmates respected and treated us fairly, helping make school a positive experience for us except for George due to his learning problems.

Relationship with The Community

There were a few white people, from the community, who in

---

[55] A remarkable coincidence is that in 1928 a Chinese laundryman's son, also named John Jung, inspired by a teacher began a correspondence with her for seven years. An archive exists of his letters. <http://www.library.und.edu/Collections/og995.html > (15 May 2005)

one way or another accepted, befriended, and helped our family. Nonetheless while they and many townspeople were friendly and liked us, our parents certainly did not have equal status relationships with whites. As children, we enjoyed somewhat more of an equal footing with our white peers at school but that standing might not have lasted through adulthood. Certainly, at times we felt we were victims of racial prejudice. If it was racial taunts or slurs, which happened once in a while, it was clear that race was the issue. But it was not always easy to know whether a specific negative encounter such as an argument or exclusionary treatment was based on racial prejudice or just due to personal dislike.

We had generally cordial relationships with blacks, mostly those who were customers. Of course, because blacks were oppressed by segregation, we did not envy their social status. As Chinese, and the only ones in town, we were neither 'fish nor fowl.' We were just different from everyone else and we learned to live with that fact.

Were We Poor?

Despite the impoverished physical surroundings where we lived, we felt quite secure. We did not feel particularly disadvantaged from the lack of anything. We were 'poor' in some material ways but for a long time, we didn't realize it because we had no opportunity to compare our material possessions and other resources with those of others. From our evening walks around town, looking in the show windows of Sterchi's furniture store, we realized that other people bought matching bedroom sets, with chests of drawers, nightstands, and dressers to go along with their beds. We saw that other people owned upholstered couches and armchairs, table and floor lamps and that they purchased wooden dining room sets with matching tables and chairs. In marked contrast, our home furnishings were comprised of our assorted collection of bed stands and bookcases improvised from apple crates, beat-up wood chairs, makeshift tables, and dilapidated beds, but it did not bother us as we were growing up.

We were not as concerned about material possessions as much as we were worried about financial and emotional security. We did increasingly feel out of place in Macon, being isolated from other Chinese, even though we children did not really know how life would differ if we had lived amongst other Chinese. All we knew was that when everyone else is either black or white, you often feel left out. In addition, having parents who were so unfamiliar with American customs, language, and culture was sometimes a source of frustration or even embarrassment. Yet, we did feel loved and secure within our family, understood the difficult lives our parents faced and appreciated the sacrifices they made in placing our needs above their own. So, in terms of overall satisfaction with our lives, we were never 'poor.'

6. Blacks, Whites, and Us

Historically the South was a region where whites held social power and treated racial minorities, especially blacks, unfairly and often unjustly. Gains in civil rights following the abolition of slavery were sharply curtailed in the last part of the 19th century with the passage of so-called Jim Crow laws that imposed the white advantage over blacks. These laws severely restricted opportunities for any equal status interactions between whites and blacks. In turn, these laws fostered informal conventions of racial social etiquette that demanded blacks be deferential and polite to whites whereas the opposite was not true. Thus, blacks had to address whites as 'sir' or 'ma'am' whereas whites could call blacks, 'boy' or 'girl.'

From the time of Father's first arrival in Macon as a bachelor in 1921 to 1956 when he finally left, rigid lines of racial separation between blacks and whites prevailed in a clearly segregated society. Before I was old enough to enter school, no one had to teach me about racial segregation because I could see clearly how "colored people" were treated as second-class citizens in every way imaginable even if I was too young to understand the history or reasons for the inequality.

The most widely known instance of inequality, of course, was the 'rule' that blacks had to ride in the "back of the bus." Exactly where the front of the bus ended, and the back began, depended on the ratio of white and black passengers. If white passengers were standing, it was expected that blacks seated in the "back of the bus" would relinquish their seats but they could not occupy empty seats near the front of the bus.

I learned at a young age how whites had priority over blacks in getting service in stores. For example, at the meat counter in the grocery store, you had to be waited on by the butchers. Black customers had to wait at the back behind the whites rather than stand mingled together. That simply was the Southern way in that era.[56] In the worse case, all whites that were in the store would expect to be waited on before any blacks would get served. A white person could defer and yield to a black person who had been waiting a long time, but that was not the norm.

In public areas such as stores, definite racial barriers gave favored status to whites. Thus, drinking fountains and toilet facilities were clearly labeled as 'White' and 'Colored.' At the train station or bus depot, there were separate waiting rooms designated for 'White' and 'Colored.' Schools and theatres were segregated. There were restaurants for whites only and others that served only blacks. Some white restaurants did have a separate door or window where blacks could order food to take out but they could not be served in the dining area. I was naïve about the really ugly side of racial hated and really did not know much about white supremacist organizations such as the

---

[56] An incident in Macon about 1950 involving Jackie Robinson, the first Negro baseball player in the major leagues, illustrates the extent to which racial segregation prevailed in Macon in that era. The Brooklyn Dodgers were scheduled to have a spring training exhibition game with the local Class A team, the Macon Peaches. The local authorities prohibited Robinson from playing in the game, despite his outstanding ability, simply because of his skin color. It would not be for another decade after we moved from Macon that the civil rights movement made major strides against segregationist policies in the South.

Klu Klux Klan. But one year there was a proposal to allow blacks to attend movies shown at the Rialto Theatre, a whites-only theatre.

The proposed plan was to allow "colored people" to sit in the balcony separated from the whites seated downstairs. One evening the KKK held a protest rally and peaceful march in front of the theatre. That marked the end of the proposal as it died very quickly.

Being Neither White nor Black

Since our family was the only Chinese, or even Asian, for that matter, family in town, we were treated as individuals rather than as a racial group. We were accepted as 'white' inasmuch as we could attend white schools and theaters and use white public toilet and drinking facilities. We were second-class citizens in other respects, being taunted or teased as slant-eyed foreigners with a strange sounding language and customs. We were sometimes objects of curiosity and targets of ridicule although we certainly did not suffer the severity of discrimination, or the level of violence faced by blacks. Much of the racial prejudice that we experienced was more in the form of a banal curiosity from ignorant hicks, albeit often in an insensitive manner rather than from malevolent intent. Thus, in 1908 the Macon paper announced the New Year's celebration of its Chinese colony, focusing on their 'curious edibles' from China such as 'dried fish with staring eyes,' birds nests, and other delicacies. This mocking tone toward Chinese customs encouraged racial intolerance.[57]

---

[57] Similarly, the 'Confucius say' jokes, which involve brief word puns, are fundamentally racist. Even though on the surface they honor the wisdom of the Chinese sage, the sing-song cadence of these one-liners mock the immigrants inability to speak proper English.

Figure 28 Article on 'curious' Chinese customs .26, Jan.1908 *Macon Daily Telegraph* 4A

Many whites, especially educated ones, treated us kindly and with concern. However, none of them could understand our view of the world since they knew little about Chinese values and upbringing. For the most part, our contact was superficial and their attitude was sometimes patronizing. Still, that was preferable to the ridicule,[58] hostility, or, on occasion, threats, we faced from a few townspeople.

Our Interactions with Blacks

Since segregation was prevalent in Macon, as in the rest of the Deep South, when I was growing up there in the 1940s and early 1950s, none of us had more than superficial contact with "colored

---

[58] Mother was very upset about how whites often ridiculed Chinese. For example, she told how some whites joke that Chinese built houses from the top down rather than from the ground up, an approach she felt whites did not really believe but concocted just to ridicule Chinese. She was probably right about their motives, and fortunately she never heard about the stereotype that laundrymen spit onto clothes to moisten them before ironing. A literary magazine columnist poked fun at this unorthodox method. (Martin Levin, "Ironing" *Saturday Review*, November 21 1970: 12, 14) He was less concerned about its unhygienic nature than he was that he could not figure out how the Chinese ever got the water in their mouths in the first place, how they could grin with a mouthful of water, or how they could talk with a mouthful of water. Father had a small brass water can with a pipe-like handle that he blew through to spray a fine mist of water, not spit, from the can onto shirts before ironing. That method could still be unsanitary but it was not used after machine pressing was widespread. Yet, popular accounts of Chinese laundrymen spitting to moisten clothes for ironing were perpetuated and widely accepted.

125

people" even though we were in close physical proximity every day in public places such as stores.

I did have a bit more contact with many blacks that were customers in our laundry when I helped Father. Although there was a range of literacy and education among both white and black customers, I was particularly struck by how many black customers could not sign their name, or did so very slowly, when they had to claim parcels having lost their ticket.

Many had trouble, or were completely unable to count their change. And, while I saw that the educational level of blacks was low, even as a child I realized that their deficiency was due somehow to the way Southern society treated them. I was too young to understand why segregation existed, but I sensed its unfairness and arbitrariness. And I understood all this when I was very young and not yet aware of atrocities against blacks such as lynching, police harassment, and legal injustices.

So although my contact with blacks was limited, I gained more experience dealing with them than the majority of whites did. As with white customers, there was considerable variability. Some were polite and patient, some were friendly and chatty, and a few were demanding or even rude to us because we were Chinese. Some of these rude customers may have been drinking but others may have been angry about something else and taking it out on us. This abusive behavior toward my parents in the laundry, I recognized as racist, because I never witnessed such rudeness from either white or black customers in stores run by whites.

And of course the blacks that we knew the best were the women who worked in our laundry. We only had one man employee who we hired to press dry cleaning. The women, mostly middle-aged, were poorly educated, if at all. They were also somewhat unreliable about showing up for work everyday, and they rarely stayed with us for more than several months. Our interactions with them were strictly work-related as they were much older than us children so we had no common interests to talk about with them. Besides, work breaks were brief and few, offering no chance for any meaningful conversation.

Other "colored people" we were familiar with were the bellboys who worked at the Lanier Hotel, just up the street. I don't recall ever seeing a white person employed in that capacity at the Lanier or at the Dempsey Hotel, the two largest hotels in town. The same color barrier held for red caps, or train porters. These jobs primarily involved serving white people, carrying luggage for hotel guests and train passengers.

The bellboys, actually grown men, often brought their personal laundry as well as that of hotel guests, since it was only a few hundred feet away. The bell 'captain' was a refined, rather dignified-looking, and very civil, elderly Negro. There were several younger bellboys, including a few who would sometimes harass us, perhaps more in jest, than with malice.

On a day to day basis, all we saw of "colored people" were laborers, nannies, cooks, dishwashers, bellboys, etc, because those were their "roles" in the South. There were no black salespeople, merchants, scholars, or political leaders in the larger community.

There were no black firemen,[59]civil service employees, and aside from those in black schools, no black teachers.

In school, and from library books, we learned about the outstanding achievements of Booker T. Washington and George Washington Carver, but they were the only models of Negro intellectual achievement we were provided. Interestingly, in the case of Carver or Washington, their race was glossed over as if they achieved greatness despite their racial background. Rather, most of the mass media images of black people depicted them as servants, such as Aunt Jemina and Uncle Ben, and old Uncle Remus benevolently telling folk tales to white children.

How Our Parents Taught Us to Deal with Racial Issues

Father left it to Mother to teach us about racism and how to deal with it. From an early age, Mother periodically cautioned us about how whites discriminated against Chinese. She told about some of her encounters with racism such as when white children would come by the laundry and taunt them, with chants of "Chinese eat rats!" [60]

She recited instances of violence against Chinese, including homicide, in cities all over the United States that she read about in the Chinese newspaper. Mother worried more over this issue than was warranted, but it was certainly understandable why she dwelled on these incidents involving racial hate. She wanted to protect her children

---

[59] Actually there were some 'colored' policemen who patrolled Broadway to deal with problems involving 'colored people.'

[60] This rumor may stem from the insinuation in a power laundry trade paper that Chinese laundrymen must eat rats to survive because they did laundry at such low prices. "Competition in laundry work," *National Laundry Journal*, 54, no. 5 (1905): 32.

by erring on the safe side. She urged us to avoid confrontations and to ignore racial insults because she felt we had no power to deal with hostile people.

Mother herself periodically reminded us that we were different, and warned that as Chinese, we would often be targets of racial prejudice. She did not want us to feel too comfortable from our being granted some white privileges. Mother often pointed out that the ways that whites mistreated blacks could also be directed toward us. From time to time she would remind us of historical incidents in which whites had mistreated Chinese such as how China suffered at the hands of Western nations when England forced opium into China in middle of the 19th century to destroy the will and resistance of the people to British domination.

Mother also told us, on numerous occasions, about how Father, like other Chinese immigrants, had to resort to buying false documents to enter the United States, because of the anti-Chinese attitudes of the U. S. government. I was upset, angry, and surprised that the U. S. treated Chinese so unjustly by excluding them, and no other group, from the opportunity to enter the country legally. This treatment was contrary to what we were taught in school about what a free country America was, and how it welcomed immigrants, at least from Europe, to the shores of New York. Learning about this aspect of how our family came to America was rather frightening for me, being just a small child.

I was torn between feelings of shame for being 'illegal' and fear that someday my parents would be apprehended and deported. It also bothered me because I felt that if my parents lied to enter the U. S., they were doing something wrong. Interestingly, I do not recall ever discussing these feelings with my sisters or them with me; perhaps we were all too frightened, embarrassed, or angry to talk about it. In fact, years later, after our family moved to San Francisco, I mistakenly assumed that every Chinese American of my age was also aware of the exclusionary immigration policies that led the Chinese to devise the "paper son" method of entry. But I never knew which of my friends may have had "paper son" fathers. And because of anxieties about such matters, I could not just ask them. And even if I had, how likely would the child of a "paper son" divulge such secrets? I was afraid to have a straightforward discussion about this issue with anyone, Chinese or non-Chinese. So I was stunned when I later discovered that many Chinese parents withheld information about their immigration experiences from their children, either from shame, fear, or because they did not want to burden them. I then realized that Mother may have told us these unpleasant details of her and Father's immigration experiences because she wanted to prepare us for the racial problems we could expect in the future. However admirable her intentions may have been, in one sense they backfired, at least with me. These stories often made me wish we had not been born Chinese, or at least, that we were not different from everyone else. If we had to be Chinese, why were we the *only* Chinese in town? It seemed so unfair.

We, like other groups that are targets of prejudice, were victimized by racism in more ways than one, for we sometimes acted or felt like we were not worthy of the respect of whites. On the other hand, since we mingled with whites at school, we did not feel we were 'completely' foreign or Chinese either. We began to disagree more often with some of our parents' Chinese beliefs and values that we saw as strange because we were being rewarded for accepting white standards and goals, which made it increasingly more difficult for Mother and Father to exert their influence on us.

Forming Our Chinese Identity

A major task for Mother and Father was to decide how to raise their Chinese children in an American society, with its racial attitudes that promoted white dominance over peoples of other skin colors. They knew only how children were reared in China, and they felt it was important for us to feel and know what it meant to be Chinese. Even though we may not have heard the term, *filial piety*, we did acquire the attitude embodied in that concept and always tried to honor and respect our parents. They often stressed to us the overriding importance of *li* (acting with proper etiquette) in dealing with other people.

However, we were simultaneously exposed to American influences, and our identification outside the home was definitely with American values. For example, although they did not have experiences of Christmas in China, it was clearly an important event in the United States. They did not deny us the joy of Christmas, and allowed us to buy a small tree each year to decorate, as long as we did not insist on lights, which Mother believed was a fire hazard. They did not buy us presents, but gave us spending money so we could buy gifts for each other as well as for them.

Further complicating the question of how our ethnic identity was being formed was the role of how the larger community of Macon viewed us. Even if we children wanted to be accepted as "whites," what was the reaction of whites toward us? Did they see or accept us children as 100 percent American or did they see us as foreign heathens or perhaps, as something in between?

Mother would relate to us incidents of racial prejudice she had suffered from whites on many occasions as we grew up. For example, during the war years, whites would taunt her on the street, making nonsensical sounds pretending they were speaking Chinese or they would make derogatory comments such as "Chinese eat dogs." She always cautioned us not to get into arguments or confrontations with white people. An issue of less pressing concern, because of their low status in society, was how blacks viewed us. They did not see us as fully 'white,' and some of them even treated us as inferiors to themselves, but the majority of them treated us fairly.

One memorable occasion that illustrates how we were viewed in society was the historic visit of Madame Chiang Kai-Shek, the First Lady of China, to Macon in 1943 during the height of World War II. Mei-Ling Soong, her maiden name, had lived in Macon when she was an adolescent because her two older sisters attended Wesleyan College there in the early 1900s. Their father had studied in the United States before returning to China to amass his fortune selling Bibles. Due to increasing political turmoil and unrest in China, he wanted his daughters to study where conditions were safer. Through his acquaintance with a Methodist missionary in town, William Burke, arrangements were made for the Soong sisters to come to Macon.

Madame Chiang also received her college education in the United States, starting with the women's college in Macon, Wesleyan, and then completing her Bachelor's degree at Wellesley College in Massachusetts before returning to China and eventually marrying Chiang Kai-Shek, the nationalist leader.

That is the background of this historic event in 1943 when Madame Chiang came to Macon after visiting numerous sites in the U. S. during this trip to rally support and aid for the war effort led by her husband against the Japanese. She was here to receive an honorary doctorate[61] at Wesleyan. The visit to Macon of such a prominent world figure was a major event of unprecedented proportion for this sleepy town. In fact, this trip to the U. S. also placed significant attention on immigration policy toward Chinese and probably was a factor in leading President Roosevelt to finally end the Anti-Chinese Exclusion Act of 1882.

Someone decided that we four Jung children, being the only children in town of Chinese descent, should be invited to attend the festivities. The publicity staff saw an human interest story in giving cute little Chinese children a chance to see the most influential Chinese woman of her era. We were paraded out for public display. I was only about 6, and none of it meant much to me, although the press release

---

[61] This honor was somewhat ironic. When Mei-Ling Soong was a grade school student in Macon, the Board of Education denied her admission to a white elementary school because she was considered an "alien." In the newspaper report, her name was misspelled, Miss Schoone. *Macon Daily Telegraph* September 22, 1910, 12.

Big Day For Tiny Jungs

By Mary Waller

(From The Macon Telegraph and News,
June 27)

Four little black-eyed Jungs, Mary, 12; Virginia, 9; John, 6; and George, 4, trudged back Saturday to their father's laundry, after one of the biggest days of their lives.

They could boast, and did, of having come in intimate contact with the lovely first lady of China, whom they had walked so far and stood so long in the hot sun to see.

Of course John and George were a little young to know what all the excitement was about. They ogled at the MP's, were deeply impressed by the siren which heralded Madame Chiang Kai-shek's approach at Wesleyan, and stared back at the children who stared at the four little hand-in-hand Chinese.

Not a Dull Moment

It was anything but a dull day for the two blue-suited, freshly scrubbed boys. But it was a different kind of day to Mary and Virginia. From the microphone came the voice of their idol. Unseen, as yet, they listened reverently, trim in their fresh gay prints. Even the curious stares

Virginia, Mary, George and John Jung, children of Macon's Chinese family

Figure 29 Local coverage of our encounter with Madame Chiang in 1943.

gushingly described our encounter of a few seconds with Madame Chiang as a thrill that we "tiny Jungs" had eagerly awaited. The most I recall was that it was a hot summer day, and I was more interested in was finding a shady spot than in getting a glimpse of Madame Chiang.

This incident shows that no matter how 'American' we children may have felt or wanted to be, in the eyes of others, we would always be seen as 'Chinese,' even if we hardly knew the culture of China or its language. Interestingly neither of our parents attended the event nor did they meet or pose with Madame Chiang for a photograph. They were either not invited, uninterested, or too busy in the laundry on the occasion.

Growing up in isolation from other Chinese was one matter. In addition, the lack of Chinese role models in books, magazines, or movies also limited our ability to fully understand what being Chinese in America meant. Most, if not all, of the depictions of Chinese were negative during that era. Fortunately, just by luck we managed to miss many of those racial stereotypes like Charlie Chan or Fu Manchu but certainly many people did not and they formed their impressions of us from these caricatures.

I did, however, suffer the sting of the one Chinese character that I was acquainted with as a child from reading the comic book, *Blackhawk*. This American hero was the leader of a squadron of fighter pilots, whose war adventures in each issue involved fighting villains such as the Axis powers. The squadron was multi-ethnic, with Blackhawk, the American leading a group that included a Frenchman, Dutchman, Norwegian, and even a Chinaman named Chop Chop.

All of Blackhawk's white crew members wore dark blue military uniforms, had revolvers, and piloted their own fighter planes, but Chop Chop wore Chinese-style garb, had a pigtail, buck teeth, and rode in the back seat of Blackhawk's plane. The other members used their firearms to fight the villains while Chop Chop ran around using only a meat cleaver as his weapon. Once in a long while, Chop Chop saved the day by being the hero and rescuing the others from disaster, but usually he was cast as a buffoon. He was about as good as it got in those days as far as any positive Chinese male role model.

Figure 30 Chop Chop, the Chinese member of Blackhawk's crew

Chinese female characters were even less frequently portrayed and never in a positive way. Thus, the only Chinese woman in a comic strip I saw was the sinister "dragon lady," from *Terry and the Pirates*. Consequently, it should be no surprise that I was conflicted about being identified as Chinese as I was growing up learning of these connotations.

When I was growing up in the 1940s, most, if not all, of the people in the adult roles that children admire such as famous historical figures, movie stars, athletes, and celebrities were white. As a young child, this lack did not really bother me. I was not concerned that my heroes such as Ben Franklin, Abe Lincoln, Thomas Edison, Charles Lindberg, Babe Ruth, and Albert Einstein, to name a few, were all white.

The stories of their lives and the levels of their achievements impressed me, and they served as models for me to look up to. However, as I became an adolescent, I did begin to secretly wish that there were some Chinese Americans who were super athletes, entertainment stars, or public leaders. I probably eventually resigned myself to this situation, reasoning that the percentage of Chinese in the population was so small that it was unlikely there could be Chinese with outstanding success stories. I did not understand how much racial prejudices also contributed to these absences.

However, eventually I learned of some isolated examples of Chinese who had made outstanding achievements in business, science, literature, and even sports. There was a Chinese businessman, Joe Shoong, who acquired considerable wealth as owner of a large chain of dry goods stores, National Dollar Stores (even though it was rumored that he exploited his employees), Norman Kwan who played professional football in Canada, Jade Snow Wong, the author and ceramic artist, and Francis Hsu, an anthropology professor. I would be filled with pride to discover that these Chinese were so successful in America.

When I was an undergraduate at Berkeley in the late 1950s, I was amazed, and indeed thrilled, that the starting fullback for the California Bears, Pete Domoto, was a Japanese American. I would have been more excited if he had been a Chinese American,[62] but I had to be satisfied that someone of Asian descent was a pioneer. Still, these outstanding models of Asian descent were few and far between. In those days, there were no Chinese super achievers like the recent ones in athletics; Michelle Kwan, Bruce Lee, Michael Chang, Yao Ming; the arts, Yo-Yo Ma, Maxine Hong Kingston, Amy Tan, architecture; I. M. Pei, Maya Lin, science; David Ho, Steven Chu, and politics; Hiram Fong, Gary Locke.

Growing up, I hate to admit it now, but there were times when I truly wished that I were *not* the child of immigrants. For being the child of immigrants meant that you were painfully different from everyone else. It was a difficult situation for both children and parents. Although I generally regarded my parents' plans for me as well intentioned, I often viewed them as obsolete or irrelevant. I thought they just didn't understand what was important and that they were hopelessly foreign. This was a painful situation, for I loved and respected my parents, but felt I was 'stuck' with them. I thought it was my bad luck to have been the child of immigrants.

---

[62] Peoples in America from different Asian backgrounds such as China, Japan, Korea, etc., were not viewed as a valid collective Asian-American entity when I was growing up anymore than one would combine French, English and Germans as European-American. The pan ethnic concept, Asian American, was a politically practical creation of the civil rights activists that overlooks major differences among its constituent members.

As I was growing up, I regarded my mother as someone who had good intentions but suffered from lack of education and knowledge about the world. I loved her but viewed her as a superstitious and ignorant person. Since I knew more than she did about history, geography, literature, etc., I arrogantly felt superior. This immaturity led me to discount or disregard much of her advice.

Whether my mother fully recognized my sentiments, I do not know, but it certainly must have been painful for her to be rejected by me. She was sacrificing everything, working all day at difficult work, and caring for her children who in turn not only did not often comply with her wishes, but also actually rejected many of her views. Yet, placed in the situation she was in, her family was literally all she had, and she surely could see that we were more and more Americanized with each day.

Mark Twain, speaking of his father, noted that when he was about 18 he viewed his father as the dumbest person who ever lived, or something to that effect. However, Twain quipped that within a few years, it was amazing how much of a turnaround his father had made. In many ways, when I was a kid I felt toward my mother the same way that Twain did about his father. Only later as an adult, did I realize and appreciate what a difficult life my mother had, and how much she had achieved through sheer determination and persistence.

Father was generally less emotional than Mother, and this was also true in dealing with children. He left most of the upbringing of the children to Mother. He would be more indulgent with us while Mother had the role of disciplinarian and reminder of our chores and responsibilities. Consequently if we wanted spending money, we would usually seek it from Father rather than from Mother.

It must have been difficult for my parents to watch us grow up, because with each successive year, each of us became more American and less Chinese. We increasingly questioned some of their plans and expectations for us because our experiences were different from theirs. We had white schoolmates and playmates, and of course, no Chinese friends or age mates. We liked English and American customs. We may have even tried to avoid thinking or behaving in Chinese ways to try to fit in. We didn't really have any choice, as there were simply no Chinese with whom we could socialize.

If Chinese playmates had been available, our parents might have wanted us to spend more time with them than with white or black children. In fact, one summer a local white missionary, who had adopted a Chinese boy about a year older than I, came to the laundry to try to establish a friendship between her son and I. We tried to play together a few times but did not get along too well and our association soon ended.

Our Chinese Consciousness

Our parents constantly reminded us of our 'Chinese-ness' in a very positive way. They told us of the history of China, and how it was a great and successful civilization over thousands of years, although it had suffered from some inept emperors who were responsible for the country's downfall in modern times. At the same time, they warned us that whites, especially, were prejudiced against us simply because we were Chinese.

We learned in school about the great achievements of Chinese civilization and it made us proud to be Chinese. Educated whites, especially our schoolteachers, who were knowledgeable about the many contributions of China over the course of history, conveyed to us that we, as Chinese, should be very proud of our cultural heritage.

As far as the practice of Chinese customs was concerned, there were limits as to what we could experience given that we were the only Chinese family around for 100 miles. Unlike communities with larger Chinese populations where they celebrated Chinese New Year with a parade complete with a dragon or lion dance and shooting of firecrackers, isolated in Macon we never knew of such customs.

In fact, the only time we saw firecrackers was on the day the war with Japan ended. To celebrate, Father lit a string of tiny red firecrackers that he placed on the end of a pole and held in front of the laundry. Similarly, we did not know about Chinese restaurants, its décor, furnishings, and of course, its cuisine. Thus we had never heard of or tasted char sui bow, dim sum, roast pig, won ton, tofu, chow mein, moon cakes, and certainly not fortune cookies, which were invented in the U. S. and unknown in China.

Our isolation in Georgia from other Chinese people produced some interesting reactions whenever we did happen to meet Chinese people. On such occasions, there was much mutual staring as we felt like we had to look again to be certain the other persons were really Chinese. Each of us felt compelled, or obligated, to approach the other to ask who they were, where they came from, and why they were there? We did not intend rudeness but acted more out of eagerness to interact with other Chinese.

Uncle Joe and Our Chinese Identification

One major link or tie to a Chinese identity for us children was our Uncle Joe who had come to America with Father's financial assistance. Uncle Joe, whose Chinese name was Jew Shiu Dun, was five years younger than Father. Like many other Chinese, he was a "paper son" who had assumed the surname of his "paper father." Thus, whereas my father was named Jung, Uncle's paper surname was Jew.[63] He also operated a laundry, but it was in Atlanta, the state capital, which was about 100 miles north of Macon. Unlike my father's situation, Uncle was separated from his wife and 3 sons who were still in China. When Chinese emigrated, some men left their families behind in China for different reasons, legal, financial, or even cultural. In addition, it would have been more difficult to survive in the U. S. initially if the immigrant also had to take care of a family. Besides, in the Chinese family, a man's wife had daughter-in-law roles to fulfill for her mother-in-law in China who held a position of power over her. In Uncle's case, he had to apply for entry as a "paper son," and it was possible that in using this fake identity, he could not also claim his real family. In any event, his family was unable to come to America until around 1950 but not without Uncle seeking the assistance of some state legislator to expedite matters.

---

[63] While our American surname is Jung, our true surname is Lo (another form is Lau). When dealing with non-Chinese, we never bothered to try to explain the discrepancy. But if a Chinese asked if we might be related to someone named Jung, we might tell them our true name if we felt we could trust them.

Not having his own family with him in Atlanta, Uncle would come by train to visit us every few months on a Sunday. This was very exciting for us, not only to see an uncle who was very indulgent and eager to see his nieces and nephews, but because he was a Chinese. He always dressed in a suit and wore a necktie when he came so we really were impressed. This was especially true since Father never wore a suit, although we had a photograph of him as a young man all dressed up. So by comparison to our contacts with Uncle, Father seemed like a country hick who wore simple everyday work clothes. The fact that Uncle always brought a pound box of Whitman's chocolates for us also did a lot to put him in high esteem. Late in the afternoon, we would walk with him several blocks to see him off at the train station for the two to three hour trip back to his laundry in Atlanta. At departure time, he would give us each a dollar, ensuring that we would be eagerly awaiting his next visit.

Once in a while Father would take me, and sometimes my sisters, on the train to Atlanta to visit Uncle in his laundry on Capital Avenue, not too far from the State Capitol building. I cannot recall Mother ever going on any of these trips. One reason was that train rides would have nauseated her. They certainly were unpleasant for me with the jerky ride of the coal-burning locomotive driven trains. The old seats in the drab Central of Georgia rail coaches had a musty smell and the train made frequent jerky stops at small towns like Barnesville, Forsyth, Griffin, before finally reaching Terminal Station in downtown Atlanta. By the time we got there after over two hours, I was nauseated. As soon as I could get off the train, I rushed to the side of the tracks and vomited and immediately felt fine. I am surprised that I was willing to take these trips, given the frequency of these unpleasant and somewhat embarrassing experiences.

Figure 31 Uncle's store, Loo Ling Laundry, was demolished for parking for Fulton County Stadium in 1966 forcing him to move around the corner to open Joe's laundry on Georgia Ave. Now operated by his grandson in 2005, it is one of the few Chinese laundries left anywhere. Ironically, it outlasted the stadium, replaced in 1996 by Turner Stadium.

It was not until the Central of Georgia Railway began operating trains with diesel locomotives such as the Nancy Hanks II about 1950 that I enjoyed train rides. This deluxe air-conditioned train left Macon around 11:30 a.m. and arrived in Atlanta about 1:30. That schedule gave us several hours to visit Uncle Joe and other Chinese who had laundries before we had to go back to the train station by 6 p.m. for the two-hour return trip to Macon.

A primary reason why Mother almost never took these trips was that she would not have had much to do during the visit. She would not have much to discuss with Uncle or other Chinese men in Atlanta. Father sometimes also squeezed in a short visit to a second cousin, Mon Kow Cheung, who had a laundry in another part of town near the stadium of the Atlanta Crackers baseball team. This family had five children close in age to us, so that we would socialize with them for an hour or two. On her few visits there, Mother had only a brief opportunity to socialize with Mon Kow's wife, Ng Shee, before it would be time to head to the train terminal to catch the train home.

In retrospect, the trips should have been really boring even to me. During the typical visit, the two brothers would sit in the laundry next to Uncle's bachelor sleeping quarters and gossip about relatives or discuss worldly matters that I didn't fully comprehend. These visits were nonetheless exciting for me, because Atlanta was a much larger city than Macon, and I was impressed by the many tall buildings, large downtown area, and domed state capitol building.

One summer when I was about 10, Father allowed Jean and me to stay for over a week in Atlanta with Uncle Joe. He relinquished his small, enclosed sleeping area in the laundry to us while he slept on a cot in the back of his store. This visit was very exciting for us and he was also delighted to have our company. During the day, Uncle worked but we took the bus to visit the exhibits in the State Capitol building, which was straight up the street about a mile, and to shop in downtown stores with spending money he gave us. When we returned, he cooked dinner for us. This memorable visit with him further endeared Uncle Joe to us.

Figure 32 Uncle Joe with the Jung children, c. 1946

Although the more typical one-day visits with Uncle Joe in either Macon or Atlanta were widely separated in time, they gave us children a stronger Chinese identity than we could have ever formed in Macon where there were no other Chinese. Aside from a few soldiers of Chinese ancestry stationed at Camp Wheeler during the war or an occasional exchange student from China attending one of the local colleges, we never had encountered another Chinese person. Whenever possible, Mother and Father extended invitations to them for dinner to be hospitable which also provided us children with rare chances to meet other Chinese.

On our visits to Atlanta to visit Uncle, we sometimes met a few other Chinese laundrymen. Listening to their conversations about other Chinese men from their home villages running laundries in towns in several southern states, I formed the erroneous impression that all Chinese in America ran laundries. After all, as noted earlier my father, his brother, and two cousins all owned laundries while other relatives from the village in China operated laundries in Chattanooga, Birmingham, and one or two other southern towns like Talladega. In fact, according to a directory that my parents had listing all the known Chinese-owned businesses in the South, most Chinese seemed to run either laundries or small grocery stores. The large extent to which Chinese engaged in laundries as a livelihood seemed curious to me as I was growing up, but I had no idea why such was the case. But, given the necessity of new immigrants getting help from relatives from their Chinese villages that were already established in the South, it really should not be surprising that so many Chinese from my father's village ended up living in the same region and entering the same business.

On one of my visits to Atlanta I encountered my first Chinese restaurant, Ding Ho, on Luckie Street. I was impressed since a Chinese restaurant[64] had a much more attractive interior than the inside of a Chinese laundry. The dining room, full of neatly arranged chairs and tables with clean tablecloths as well as Chinese art decorating the walls, greatly impressed me. I think I was also relieved just to know that Chinese did operate businesses other than laundries.[65] However, this

---

[64] Chinese restaurants did not become widespread and popular with non-Chinese until after the laundries were well-established. Their popularity grew and continued to prosper long after the Chinese laundries disappeared. Chinese restaurant cooks acquired culinary skills while employed as houseboys, cooks, and servants in white homes or restaurants. Success in this endeavor, like that in laundries, showed how adaptable the immigrants were in surviving in a society hostile to their presence.

[65] Legend has it that some whites demanded food late one evening at a Chinese restaurant. The cook tossed together some left-over ingredients to appease them. They loved the stir-fried concoction. "Chop suey," roughly translated as "odds and ends" helped popularize Chinese food and came to represent the epitome of Chinese cuisine for many whites, although no self-respecting Chinese would ever order such a lowly dish.

was only a social call for my father to gather with the men working in the restaurant, and not a dining occasion; it was still several years before I actually got to eat a full meal in a Chinese restaurant and discover the wonderful cuisine of Canton. The waiters made a big fuss over me, as Chinese love young children. They even offered me some food, a dish that had lobster in it. I had never seen or tasted lobster before, but the food looked and smelled quite appealing. I bit into the hard shell of a piece of lobster, not realizing that you were supposed to eat the meat inside the shell, and thus my initial encounter with Chinese restaurant food was rather unpleasant.

The Chinese are notorious for their love of gambling. In Atlanta, a family association raised funds to provide a meeting and social hall on the second floor of a building on Whitehall Street not far from the train terminal. It also served as a place where the old, and not so old, Chinese men would congregate from nearby small towns on Sundays, their day off from work, to gamble and socialize.[66] From Mother, I later learned that Father also engaged in this activity but I was too young to notice or remember. From Mother's accounts over the years, I learned that he indulged in the vice more than she liked. Although he eventually stopped going to the gambling hall, she liked to cite his gambling habit when she wanted to complain to us about his

---

[66] It is only a conjecture but bonds formed through these social interactions may be why some Chinese who died in other cities were brought to Atlanta for burial in the Chinese section of Greenwood cemetery. Such was the case for one of my distant relatives who died in Chattanooga in 1969 even though none of his immediate kin lived in Atlanta.

bad habits. Being very young at the time when I made those visits with him, I did not know what gambling was, or that it was a bad activity.

There was one occasion that I do recall vividly when Father had taken me to the meeting hall. While he gambled, I sat by idly in a corner patiently waiting for him to take me home to Macon. An elderly Chinese man befriended me, and when he learned I did not know how to count in Chinese, he proceeded to teach me how to count to 100. It only took a few minutes to acquire this new skill, but the lesson has lasted. This fond memory was proof that I made at least one visit with Father to the Chinese gambling hall in Atlanta.

Parents' Reminders of China

I don't recall our parents ever talking much about China to us, unless we pressed them for details about their lives in China. They tried to satisfy our curiosity but they didn't have much to tell us other than that they came from small villages with farm animals. Still, they did have a large fold-up map of China, which I recall was, appropriately, colored yellow. Father would unfold and lay it open across the bed to show us how large China was and where Canton, as it was called then, the nearest large city to their villages, was located. It was exciting to look at the map even though we had never been there because it provided a feeling of connection with our parents' origins.

There were two photographs of relatives in China that our parents displayed on the wall next to their bed. One, shown in Figure 33, was sent from China probably in the early 1940s, showing paternal grandmother, Uncle Joe's wife and their three oldest sons, and third uncle and his wife with their first two daughters.

Figure 33 Relatives in China in the late 1940s. Back row: Uncle Joe's wife, Thay Woy, sons William and Hoi Lam on the right and James on far left. Next, my youngest uncle, Hok Su Lo, and his wife, Wu Fong Shui, with their two oldest daughters, York Lin and York Bing, on the left front. Paternal grandmother is seated in the center.

Figure 34 Uncle Joe's sons in China, Wei Lam, Hoi Lam, and See Lam. c. 1943.

Third uncle, Hok Su Lo, had tried to enter the United States in 1937 with Father's aid. He failed the immigration interrogation and was detained on Angel Island for almost a year before he was sent back to China. Later, he studied in Japan, but at the outbreak of war between China and Japan, he returned to China where he married and had a family with three daughters and a son. We children were curious because they were our relatives, but the interest was brief as we had never met any of them. The other photograph, shown in Figure 34, portrayed Uncle Joe's three sons in China. Although I had not met these cousins either, I was intrigued by their serious expressions and I wondered what they were like. Eventually they came to live with him in Atlanta but not until immigration issues were resolved several years after the end of World War II.

Our Family Photographs

The other framed family photograph that my parents displayed prominently was a family portrait in Figure 35 that showed them with Uncle Joe and only my sisters, as George and I were not yet born.

Figure 35 Father and Uncle, on the right, with Mother, Jean, and Mary, 1936.

Uncle and Father are neatly attired in suits and wearing neck ties, and it fascinated me because I had never seen Father dressed that way in Macon. Laundry work called for much plainer clothing and besides, we never had an occasion when Father needed such formal dress.

Our parents had a black photograph album containing pictures Father took of us children and them as we grew up using a Kodak camera, the type with a bellows that collapsed and closed when you folded it. Most of the poses were in front of the laundry, in the park across the street, or on downtown streets. A few were sent to relatives in China and we received photographs of them in exchange. Some evenings we enjoyed looking at the photographs with our parents to see how we were changing as we grew up.

Years later, we discovered other formal photographs of both Mother and Father taken about the time when they married. They were stored away and we never saw them when we were children, discovering them only after our parents had died. Sadly, because we never met any of our grandparents, we never saw photographs of them until they were obtained from other relatives when we were much older.

Planning a Chinese Future for Their Children

In occasional family conversations, my parents would discuss their future plans, and how they hoped to return to live in China when they retired. We would always object immediately to any plans to move us to China, saying that we would refuse to leave with them because we were Americans and wanted to stay here.

Eventually, with the fall of Chiang Kai-Shek and the nationalist Chinese government in 1949 to Mao Zedong and the communists, relations between the U. S. and China were disrupted. The prospect of any of us going to China anytime soon vanished. I think it was then that my parents more or less resigned themselves to spending the rest of their lives in the U. S.

I was only 12 then but I was quite upset that the Communists were ruling China, because we were taught in school that Chiang Kai Shek and the Kuomintang was the legitimate government. After all, the United States favored and supported Chiang as an ally, hero, and great leader during the fight against the Japanese invasion of China. I did not know then that widespread corruption prevailed in Chiang Kai Shek's regime. I was somewhat shocked when my parents saw benefits in the change of power even if it created problems for their own plans to return to China. Mother always said that when your country is weak, other nations despise you and treat you with contempt. Only when your country is strong, she argued, will they give you respect.

Because the Communists and the People's Republic of China were successful in becoming a world power, my parents felt that Chinese in America would not face as much scorn and prejudice. However, as a child raised in America, it was troubling to see the Chinese nationalist party, the ally of the U. S., lose to the communists. Since the communists were enemies of the U. S., I was afraid that we would now face worse treatment simply because we were Chinese.

I held these anxieties even though I, as a child, was totally unaware of how innocent Japanese Americans were distrusted and placed in internment camps during World War II. Actually, no one in our family experienced any direct problems due to this political situation but many Chinese either were worried or had actually been harassed, or even deported during the late 1950s. The U. S. government suspected that they might be spies or sympathizers of Communist China and might become traitors.[67] [68] This period was the heyday of Senator Joe McCarthy and the House On Un-American Activities Committee, so there was good reason to be afraid of being viewed as disloyal to America. But if my parents were worried about this backlash, they kept it to themselves.

When my older sisters reached adolescence, Mother was very strict about whom they hung around with and what time they had to be home. In part, this reflected the greater concern that parents generally have about the safety of their daughters, but it also stemmed from Mother's fear that we would date and eventually marry whites. My older sister, Mary, spent a lot of her time after school with her girlfriends at their homes a few blocks away. Preoccupied with her white or *lo fan* school friends, she would lose track of time occasionally, and not get home until after dark, and she would catch hell from Mother. Mary would come up the front stairs, usually after dark

---

[67] The FBI harassed Chinese laundrymen in New York City implicated with leftist organizations. Because they were of Chinese heritage, they were suspected of giving aid to Communist China which became an opponent of the U. S. during the Korean war. See Chapter 7, RenqiuYu, "*To Save China, to Save Ourselves: The Chinese Hand Laundry Alliance of New York* " (Philadelphia, PA.: Temple University Press, 1992)

[68] A first-person account of how the 1950's communist scare made life difficult for a paper son who operated a Chinese laundry. Tung Pok Chin, and Winifred C. Chin, "*Paper son: One man's story*" (Philadelphia, PA.: Temple University Press, 2000)

around dinner time, but could not get in unless someone inside opened the door as it had no lock that could be opened with a key from the outside. For safety, day or night, we always barricaded the front door from inside with a long iron bar placed horizontally between braces on each side of the back of the door.

As part of Mother's penalty, Mary had to wait until Mother was ready to mete out additional punishment. After about 20 or 30 minutes she relented and opened the door, loudly scolding Mary for staying out late while directing several sharp blows to Mary's legs with the handle of a broom. Mary had little choice but to cower on the stairs and endure her punishment before she could enter our living quarters. I was six years younger and didn't understand why one would disobey parents. I felt very badly for Mary, on the one hand, as I listened to her sobbing, but then I couldn't understand why she brought this punishment upon herself on repeated occasions so I must have felt she more or less deserved her fate. Jean probably felt much the same, and we couldn't understand why Mary never seemed to learn.

Jean managed to avoid this predicament. Being three years younger, she was not yet at an age where she was prone to stay out after school with her friends. Also, perhaps because she was more obedient, she did not incur the wrath of Mother. In fact, she was very successful in school and when she graduated from high school she was selected to be the class valedictorian. We were all very proud, even though we, especially my parents, were not entirely sure what it all meant. The graduation ceremony, held one evening in the Macon civic auditorium, was an exciting moment. The graduates paraded in while the band played a march worthy of a coronation. At the appropriate time in the ceremony, Jean stood up at the lectern and delivered her inspirational speech to the graduating class and the audience. It must have been exciting for Mother and Father, even though they probably did not even understand very much of what she was saying.

Sojourners No More

Many factors conspired to restrict the assimilation of my parents to American customs. On one hand, even if they wanted to become 'Americans,' the racial attitudes against Chinese made it difficult for them to be fully accepted socially. Moreover, in the back of their minds, they had always intended to return to China eventually and certainly by the time they retired.[69] Indeed, some of the money that Father sent to his family over the years was used to build a house for his youngest brother and his family to live in, with the understanding that eventually Father and Mother, and maybe even the rest of us would also live there.

However, as we children grew up, they soon realized that we saw ourselves as more American than Chinese and would not consent to live in China. This factor, itself, made it less likely that they would actually leave America upon retiring. Then with the rise of Communist

---

[69] Unlike most immigrant groups, Chinese did not readily assimilate to American values. Many left wives and children behind, intending to come only as sojourners, returning after making their fortune. Many owed money borrowed to buy papers and passage to the U. S. Racial prejudice against them in the U. S. also reinforced their lasting ties to China. Despite the infrequent correspondence forced by World War II, Chinese maintained their loyalties to their families in China. But with the rise in 1949 of the Communist regime, it became more difficult as well as dangerous for Chinese in America to send money to their Taishan families. This situation took its toll. Some unions dissolved as some wives left behind in China remarried when it seemed their husbands were unlikely to return, and some husbands in America took secret second wives. Hsu, 2000.

China in 1949, the possibility of ever returning became even less likely. Some years later, during the People's Republic land reform policy, the government confiscated privately-held property. Our parents no longer had any choice but to live the rest of their lives in the United States.[70]

Was there any good future for a Chinese family in Macon, Georgia? As the *only* Chinese in the region, Mother and Father felt the loneliness of cultural isolation. They neither wanted to nor could ever be fully American while their children could never be fully Chinese. Although their children possessed Chinese physical features, their cultural and social upbringing was decidedly American.

They realized an urgent need to move the family to California when my sisters reached adolescence. In San Francisco, because of its large Chinese population, our parents hoped their daughters could meet, and hopefully marry, Chinese boys. If they remained in Macon, we children might enter mixed-race marriages, which my parents did not consider desirable. They also knew that mixed-race marriages and any offspring would meet great hostility, especially in the South.

Mother insisted that the family should move to San Francisco so that we children could meet more Chinese people, and learn the values, customs, and culture of China. A plan was devised to move to San Francisco in stages. Father was to stay behind in Macon for some unknown time to operate the laundry to provide us a steady income. Mary, as the oldest child was to leave first, accompanied by Mother.

---

[70] The changing post WWII political situation in China caused conflicts of loyalties for many immigrants. Chinese suspected of allegiances to Red China suffered new tensions. Xiaojian Zhao, "*Remaking Chinese America: Immigration, family, and community, 1940-1965*" (New Brunswik, N. J.: Rutgers University Press, 2002)

Immediately upon Mary's graduation from high school in 1949, Mother escorted her by rail across the country to San Francisco where she entered college that fall.

Mother also had the difficult task of locating a piece of property in San Francisco that would provide rental income as well as living quarters above it for our family residence. This task needed prompt action because the following year, Jean, George and I were to make the move from Macon. In view of Mother's limited English skills and lack of financial experience, especially in dealing with real estate, the difficulty of the challenge was immense. Fortunately, James Loo, a Chinese friend of the family who had years ago attended college in Macon now lived in San Francisco, and offered to help her find competent Chinese realtors.

Jean and I were both excited and scared about the move. The prospect of having a real house to live in rather than the space above the laundry was appealing. We had a Sears Roebuck catalog that we perused to fantasize about the furnishings we would buy. I sketched floor plans of our imagined home. Still, the thought of suddenly moving over 3,000 miles away to a place we had never been was rather frightening. I recall that I myself was not immediately pleased at the thought of leaving Macon and my school friends. After all, I was only 14 and Macon was the only place I had known. I am certain George and Jean also had some doubts as well. San Francisco was just a dot on the map as far as I was concerned and I could not foresee any benefits or advantages of living among thousands of other Chinese as compared to staying in Macon.

7. Our New Lives in San Francisco

The journey by train from Georgia to San Francisco was long, taking almost three days. First Mother and Mary went from Macon to Atlanta where they boarded an overnight train to Chicago. Arriving at the Dearborn Street Station, they transferred to the Chicago Northwestern Station to board a transcontinental train that transported them to California. During the layover of several hours between trains in Chicago, Mother left Mary to wait in the cavernous train station and headed out into the streets of downtown Chicago in search of food to bring onto the train to last for the entire trip. Meals served on trains were expensive. A short while later she reappeared at the train station loaded with enough bread and lunchmeats to feed them during their two-day trip west.

Mother remained in San Francisco for several months to help Mary get settled there before she returned to Macon. Mary enrolled in a community college, City College of San Francisco and rented a room at the YWCA in Chinatown on Clay Street from where it required about 30 minutes to commute to the college. She quickly became very popular with the local Chinese students, which pleased her as she was unaccustomed to the warm welcome and attention. Mary was pleased with her welcome and quickly adjusted to her new environs. She was invited to enter a beauty pageant sponsored by the Chinese Students Club at the college.

Figure 36 Mary entered the Chinese Student Club Sweetheart Ball Pageant

At City College she met her future husband, Edward Gee, who was studying electrical engineering. Not long after, they married and Mary became part of a large Chinese family as Ed had three brothers and three sisters. As newlyweds, Mary and Ed lived on Pacific Street about four blocks from where the rest of our family would eventually move to when we left Macon two years later.

They occupied one of four apartments in a building not far from Chinatown. Her parents-in-law owned the building and lived in one of the other apartments. The remaining two apartments were occupied by two of Ed's siblings, and their families. With so many in-laws living in the same building, Mary received an instant introduction to many aspects of Chinese customs and practices that we knew nothing about in Macon.

Her mother-in-law owned and operated a garment-sewing factory on the ground floor of the apartment building. At least five or six older Chinese women worked there sewing women's garments for dress designers. This type of arrangement was sometimes the only opportunity for employment for these women who spoke little or no

English. They worked long hours, often in crowded conditions for low wages. They had deadline pressures and had to work rapidly. Yet, they had a lively camaraderie among them, chattering away with lively conversation while they worked and playing mah jongg during their breaks.

Figure 37   Mary and Ed celebrate at their wedding in 1951.

Meanwhile, Mother began her mission to look for property. Only then could the rest of the family move out as well.   Coming from a small southern town to a large bustling city was a big change. Not only did she have to find an affordable property in good condition that was in a desirable location, she had to learn the basics of real estate transactions such as down payments, financing, depreciation, and return on investment. Her diligence and persistence paid off, and with the help of Chinese-speaking realtors, Mother found a property that had a six-room flat to house our family upstairs and a store beneath it that we rented to the operator of a laundromat.

When Mother and Mary left Georgia, a new chapter opened in the life of our family. It was exciting, but also frightening in some ways. With Mother in San Francisco, Jean and I had to help Father operate the laundry after school. Father prepared the meals. Somehow we survived the abrupt modification of our family structure and functions even though there were some uncomfortable moments. In particular, one night several months after Mother had gone to San Francisco, Father must have had a nightmare. We were awakened because he was screaming and crying uncontrollably because he was beginning to think that Mother had abandoned the family and was not planning to return. I was quite frightened by this incident, but Jean somehow managed to calm and reassure him. His fears were unwarranted, as Mother returned to Macon after she finalized the purchase of our new home.

So, in the summer of 1952, we began the second phase of our move with everyone heading west by rail except for Father who stayed behind to operate the laundry alone to provide continuing income for our family. There was no fanfare; he was prepared to make the sacrifice because it was for the good of the family. He was now a bachelor laundryman, just as his brother had been for over 13 years in Atlanta. Ironically, at about the same time as we were moving, Uncle Joe, who visited his family in Hong Kong in 1949, was finally successful in 1950 in gaining entry into the U. S. for his wife and three sons, and, a new fourth baby son.

As with the trip she made a few years earlier with Mary, Mother was in charge. Inasmuch as we were moving our household to California, we checked as much baggage as the railway company allowed and then each of us carried at least two other pieces of luggage onto the coach. With so much luggage there was little space left for sitting, and I spent much of the time sitting in the smoking lounge adjacent to the Men's lavatory or just walking through the train. This mobility is probably what prevented me from having the motion sickness that I had often suffered during the two-hour train trips I took with Father to visit Uncle Joe.

Just as she had done on her earlier trip across the country with Mary several years earlier, when we arrived in Chicago, Mother had us three children wait in the train station as she quickly disappeared into the crowded downtown streets of Chicago. Before long, she returned like a mother bird with sustenance for the two-day rail journey to California. Finally, we arrived at Emeryville, on the eastern edge of the San Francisco bay and the final stop on the train route. There we transferred to the ferry that would carry us across the bay to San Francisco. Almost three days ago when we left Macon, it had been over 90 degrees, but San Francisco summers are quite cool due to the fog. We shivered on the ferryboat as it slowly inched west across the bay through the dense fog. Suddenly, we saw the towering Bay Bridge, and then the hills and skyline of San Francisco emerged as we got closer to the Ferry Building at the foot of Market Street.

After one year of separation from Father, I returned to Macon during the next summer to keep him company and to help him in some small way. For three months, I helped him mainly in waiting on customers leaving or picking up laundry. It was a positive experience in many ways for both of us and it strengthened our ties to each other. After I returned to San Francisco at the end of summer, Father remained behind for three more lonely years, aside from one short visit to San Francisco in 1955. Finally, Father sold the laundry and rejoined us in San Francisco in the spring of 1956.

Figure 38 Father taking a break in the laundry. Summer, 1953.

But while Father was in Georgia and we were in San Francisco, we learned how to deal with a new physical environment as well as a new family structure. Now, Mother was in charge, and at age 15, I was the 'man of the house.' During this period of about four years without the physical presence of Father, Mother, as the head of the household, acquired a strong sense of independence. At first she searched for work in Chinatown and even tried washing dishes as well as sewing in a garment factory, but she was not fast enough to keep up with the experienced workers. She even mentioned the possibility of working on farms picking crops, but we were alarmed and discouraged her.

As luck would have it, about a year after we moved to San Francisco, the owner of the laundromat went bankrupt and offered it for sale. It fit our situation well because running a laundromat was much less demanding than operating a regular laundry. Our parents purchased it and Mother operated it herself with some help from us after school. Given Mother's limited English skills, a self-service business like a laundromat was a good choice.

Although laundromats offered and encouraged self-service, most of our customers were working people and they wanted full service. They did not have time to tend to their own laundry, but dropped it off and wanted us to wash, dry, fold, and wrap their laundry. Mother had to interact with customers much more than she did in the laundry in Macon. It was largely through these interactions with customers that she acquired sufficient command of English and felt more in control of her life.

Mother still did all of the grocery shopping and meal preparation even though she was busy running the laundromat. After a full day of work, she cooked fresh Chinese meals every night as she felt it was important for us to have nutritious meals. Whenever I had an opportunity to eat out with white friends, she would try to feed me before I left if I was planning to have American food. She believed you could not get full from *American* meals and soon afterwards you would be hungry. I was amused because I knew she was unacquainted with exactly the same criticism about Chinese food leveled by whites. And, given that she had never had an American meal herself, she had no firm basis for her advice.

Living in the flat above the laundromat saved us the time and expense of commuting to work but it was still necessary that Jean and I assist Mother in our new household and business. We often tended the store after school so she could do her other chores.

Figure 39 Mother at work in the laundromat, 1954.

Mary, although living nearby, could not help, as she was part of another family even though we saw her often. Besides, she was expecting her first child, Richard, while her husband Eddie, now serving in the Navy, was away at a base in Virginia.

Adjusting to Life in A Chinese Community

The move to San Francisco involved many adjustments, not only to geographical but also cultural changes. When Jean and I first arrived in San Francisco, like Mary a few years earlier, we really did not know how to be 'Chinese.' Although we knew we were 'Chinese,' we had little prior social contact with Chinese people in Georgia and did not possess much knowledge of Chinese customs.

In San Francisco, we had ample opportunity to develop new friendships through social contact with Chinese Americans. Most of the Chinese of my age that I met were second generation. Since their parents, like mine, were immigrants, most of them were bi-lingual in varying degree while their parents had limited English language skills or preferred to speak in Chinese. Generational conflicts were common. The first generation often disapproved of the Americanization of their children, lamenting their lack of traditional Chinese values and customs. They termed their American-born children, *jook-sing* (hollow bamboo) ridiculing how empty they were of Chinese culture and values. The children, in turn, regarded their parents as old-fashioned and were often embarrassed or ashamed to be seen with them by their friends. Few, if any, of my Chinese American friends bothered to introduce their immigrant parents to me when I visited their homes.

The challenge facing the second generation was how to walk the narrow line between the Chinese ways of their parents and the American ways of the U. S. The dilemma was that the second generation was neither 'fish nor fowl' and sometimes they felt rejected by both cultures. To adapt, they often would act more Chinese when they were with other Chinese while they behaved in less Chinese ways when they were with non-Chinese.

When we first came to San Francisco, we were not as 'Chinese' as those Chinese who grew up there because of our isolated existence in Macon. But now we were curious to learn more about what being Chinese entailed. "Chinese-ness" now became a salient aspect of our identities. One valuable aid in our cultural transition initially was the large extended family that Mary acquired through marriage. The large Gee clan was very outgoing, and warmly receptive of us. Thus, we were immersed almost overnight into Chinese life style and customs to a degree that we could not have otherwise achieved for many months. We learned about many aspects of Chinese family values, traditions, and customs firsthand from the Gee family.

Jean's Experience

Jean followed in Mary's footsteps, enrolling at City College of San Francisco, and she also joined the Chinese Student Club and entered the Chinese students' beauty pageant. Like Mary, Jean was pretty, and coming from Georgia, her southern drawl captured lots of attention from young Chinese men. She had a very busy social life, with numerous boyfriends calling her for dates.

After two years of study at City College, Jean transferred to the nearby University of California at Berkeley across the bay. She was very popular and became active with the Chinese student social organizations and quickly developed her Chinese identity. She switched her interest in nursing to education and, upon graduation, continued in this field of study at the University of Southern California.

Figure 40 Jean also entered the Sweetheart Ball pageant at City College

My Adjustment Experience

On the other hand, my adjustment to living in a Chinese community was more difficult. I was rather shy at age 15, partly because I was a skinny and self-conscious kid who was unusually tall for a Chinese at 6' 4." This led to some good-natured teasing and attention from Chinese-American students who averaged about 5' 7" for males and about 5' 2" for females.

I had some difficulty in identifying with the Chinese-American students in school, because the Chinese Americans in San Francisco seemed so different from me in many ways. Most of them had grown up in Chinatown, attended *de facto* segregated schools that were predominantly Chinese. They were influenced by Chinese customs and culture all of their lives and were thoroughly self-identified by their

Chinese heritage. They not only could speak Chinese much better than I could, but some could read and write Chinese to some extent because from an early age their parents had sent them to Chinese language school after their American school hours. But, coming from Georgia, where we were neither white nor black, we were a different breed of Chinese. For example, I was probably more willing to affiliate with students of any color or background whereas Chinese-American students in San Francisco, by choice or by necessity, isolated themselves from other ethnic groups.

I entered Lowell High School, an academically prestigious school considered by some to be the "Harvard" of high schools. My southern drawl did not have the positive impact that it had for my sisters, as it led many people to perceive me as a hillbilly or country bumpkin. Also, it was difficult for me to be just "average" after being one of the top students at my junior high school in Macon. Many of my Lowell classmates went on to become lawyers, judges, and one, Stephen Breyer, was appointed to the U. S. Supreme Court.

Adding to my distress, Mother enrolled me in a language class at a Chinese church so I could learn to read and write Chinese. Unfortunately, I was 15 years old, and my 6-year old classmates were infinitely more adept at learning Chinese than I. It was embarrassing and I quickly became a dropout.

Much worse, however, in my second year of school I tested positive on a tuberculin skin test. Although I had been exposed to tuberculosis, fortunately I was not considered an active or contagious case. Nonetheless, it was recommended that I best receive bed rest and home schooling for a year with a visiting teacher that came several days each week. I felt like I was under house arrest. Mother took it in stride, making extra efforts to prepare nutritious meals for me, while also running the laundromat. Fortunately, the next year I was cleared by my doctor to return to complete my senior year.

At Lowell, as well as other high schools with a large Chinese enrollment, Chinese students voluntarily segregated themselves and socialized mainly with Chinese. I hesitantly conformed, trying to limit my social contacts to other Chinese, but it seemed awkward for me, coming from Macon where everyone I knew at school had been white. It was not that I did not want to socialize with Chinese as much as I did not want to restrict myself to Chinese friends. Also, I think I was ambivalent about being identified as Chinese. The racist stereotypical images of Chinese that emphasized slanted eyes, straight hair, queues, sing-song Chinese music and spoken language, idiographic Chinese written characters, and exotic clothing items like coolie hats had subtly poisoned my desire to identify as Chinese.

Adding to the difficulty of my adjustment from a region where no one else was Asian to one with Asians from many countries was that I found it difficult to distinguish Chinese from other Asians. Thus, I could not readily identity students of Chinese from those of Japanese descent. This matter was important to me when it came to dating because at that time students of Chinese and Japanese origin did not mingle much because their parents would object. The 1950s were too close in time to the invasion of China by Japan during World War II.

Although I had trouble separating Chinese Americans from

Japanese Americans by physical features, I finally discovered an easier method. Surnames were an easy and valid cue as most Chinese surnames had one syllable and most Japanese surnames contained two or three syllables. Of course, attitudes changed over time and with the civil rights activism of the 1960s, both groups worked together as "Asian Americans," along with peoples from other Asian cultures, to achieve common political purposes.

Outside of school I spent much time socializing with other Chinese American youth at a community center in Chinatown closely connected with the Chinese Presbyterian Church. Cameron House, which in the early history of Chinatown had been a refuge for Chinese women rescued by missionaries from enforced lives of prostitution, offered many recreational and social opportunities for Chinatown youth. From these informal contacts, I came to better understand what it meant to be Chinese American.[71] Being around and accepted by other Chinese of my own age for the first time validated my Chinese identification. I began to attach greater positive value to my ethnicity than previously, to such an extent that I recall that I was disturbed whenever I met a Chinese with mixed race parentage. Because society frowned on interracial dating and mixed marriage, I felt sorry for the plight of these bi-racial offspring and it helped me appreciate why my parents wanted us to marry other Chinese.

When I graduated from high school, I did not have a career focus. I more or less wasted a year at City College of San Francisco

---

[71] There was a large social and cultural separation between ABC or American Born Chinese and the FOB or Fresh Off The Boat Chinese. Like other ABCs, I did not interact much with FOBs. ABCs tended to feel superior to FOBs and avoided them.

where I enrolled mainly because my friends were going there. Uninspired there, I had no sense of direction and the lack of interest in academics among my friends was not helpful. Fortunately, after one year there, at Jean's urging, I transferred to the University of California in Berkeley where the intellectual atmosphere was far more challenging. I completed my B.A. degree there, with a major in psychology.

George's Adjustment

It was no surprise that it was more difficult for George to adjust when we moved to the much larger and different environs of San Francisco. He was now 14 years old entering adolescence. I think he certainly increased his awareness of what being Chinese meant, as we lived on the edge of Chinatown, which was decidedly different from Macon. George understood and knew how to speak Chinese to a small extent, adequate for family communication, but it was not sufficient for conversing with other Chinese people.

San Francisco schools were not any more successful in helping meet George's needs than the ones in Macon. George still had problems with school. Eventually, the school decided vocational training of some sort was the only alternative and placed him in some type of work situation near Chinatown. His first job required unloading merchandise. He hated it, and his supervisor, and soon quit. Eventually I got him to help me with my early morning newspaper delivery route for the San Francisco Examiner. Next I got him an afternoon paper route on Nob Hill, and helped him deliver the San Francisco News Call-Bulletin.

None of these activities had any long-range promise. George

soon just stopped going to school completely. There was little guidance from the schools, and Jean and I were too busy with our own education and lacked the knowledge of possible alternative education for George. Mother, meanwhile, sheltered George so that anytime we would urge him to explore new employment, he would balk knowing that Mother would protect and defend him. He had no interest in working nor did he have any marketable skills. He could read and write to some extent, mainly acquired from his interest in movies and television that motivated him to read programming advertisements.

George was unkempt in his appearance and attire, and increasingly so as he got older. He was very rigid, preferring only a certain style or type of clothing. For example, cotton plaid shirts and gray work pants became his favorite attire. At some point he gave up wearing shoes, preferring to use his slippers on the street as well as at home.

George, roaming the neighborhood became friendly with many merchants and employees in stores along Polk Street. People liked George; they realized that his mental capacity was limited but although childlike in his trust of and openness to strangers, he was nonetheless shrewd in judging them and instinctively knew whom to approach and whom to avoid. Soon he was spending hours at Woolworth's dime store where although not employed, he volunteered to help with moving merchandise. The employees indulged and tolerated him, and he felt accepted there.

George gradually expanded his exploration of the city. When some of his Polk Street acquaintances moved to work in other parts of town, he rode buses to visit them. Years later when monthly bus passes were introduced George went and explored the city wherever a bus route would take him. He knew all the routes and how to get to any location in the city. At home he spent most of his time watching television. When he went out, it was anyone's guess where he was headed. He would come home with all manner of items, stuffed animals, advertising flyers, and business brochures -- things he got from stores or found discarded on the street during his meanderings.

Despite his poor school abilities George surprised with how much he could learn when he was interested. He learned to play chess, which he found fascinating, even if he never developed complex strategies. If I could not be enticed to play, he would spend hour after hour playing against himself. Years later, when computer chess games became available, we bought him one. He has been playing chess against the computer every day for at least the past 30 years.

George always had a healthy appetite, and usually ate like the proverbial horse. Mother indulged him, and even encouraged him to eat large portions. He was set in his food preferences, preferred only a few, favorite dishes, and was reluctant to eat anything new. When he was young, he was thin despite his diet, but in middle age, he gained weight and although not obese, he became flabby. He maintained relatively good health probably because he did so much walking around San Francisco.

When Father or I tried to cajole or coax George to do various things he would not cooperate. Over time, he grew very negative, and would argue with Father especially when he criticized George, who would loudly sass him back. Mother always intervened and protected George, who knew he could always count on her backing. Of course, she too would become impatient and scold him for his lack of effort or his gluttonous eating. He did not like to hear such comments, but coming from Mother, he would ignore or even laugh them off.

Gradually, George's stuffed animals, toy soldiers, toy autos, and movie memorabilia crammed the Polk Street flat. He rummaged through street garbage cans. He brought home advertising flyers from stores, as product promotion displays, cigarettes and candy racks, and samples of deodorant, soaps, and toothpaste. If it was not nailed down, and was free or being discarded, it was for George. Since Mother also had hoarding proclivities, the flat had little empty space.

Mother's Adjustment

Mother had had few opportunities to socialize with any Chinese, men or women, since she had left China over 20 years before.[72] In fact, this lack of opportunity probably contributed to her never really developing any close social bonds with other Chinese even after she moved to San Francisco. Perhaps the years of being suspicious and distrustful of strangers during her solitary existence in Georgia may have contributed to her reticence to foster social ties.

---

[72] Mother was, of course, not the only Chinese woman in the South who was isolated from contact with other Chinese women. I knew directly of only two other Chinese women raising families in the South, my uncle's wife, Thay Woy and Ng Shee, the wife of father's cousin, Sang Bok. I assumed that since they lived near each other they would have many interactions. In fact, both had restricted social lives. Ng Shee was raising five children and helping out in the laundry. Thay Woy was also busy raising three sons, and later helping with five grandchildren. While the men could gather at the Chinese association hall in Atlanta to gossip or gamble, their wives stayed home to look after young children and prepare meals. I heard stories of other Chinese women in the South who were similarly isolated from each other. The situation might have been better in Augusta where there were more Chinese families.

Mother always seemed to be uncomfortable in social settings where people engage in idle chit-chat. Her heavy workload in Macon had rarely given her free time for such activities.

Mother's experience in the Chinese community was quite different from ours, of course, because she was already an adult. And, having grown up in China, already knowing how to speak Chinese and being familiar with Chinese customs, the transition was much easier for her. After being in Macon for so many years, it was a refreshing experience for her to deal with Chinese-speaking merchants and shop for food in stores that carried Chinese produce, cuts of meat, and ingredients.

Chinatown Encounters

The center of San Francisco's Chinatown was a curious blend of stores that served the needs of the Chinese, and curio shops, boutiques, and restaurants that catered to the Caucasian tourist trade. Many Chinese lived in crowded housing within a few blocks of this commercial area that was concentrated along Grant Avenue between Pacific and Bush Streets.

In the 1950s, Chinese people could not easily buy real estate or move out of Chinatown. Most lived between Kearney Street to the East and Leavenworth or Hyde Streets to the West, with Broadway the northern boundary and Sacramento Street the southern boundary.

Our family lived on the outskirts of what was the Chinese community when Polk Street was several blocks beyond the western perimeter of the major Chinese community. Thus, Mother was a pioneer of sorts, as few Chinese had acquired property as far west of

Chinatown as Polk Street because of racial discrimination. It was a sedate, safe, and clean area, with a small town feel, contained a variety of businesses including hardware stores, groceries, a five and dime store, two movie theatres, and some restaurants. There were few Chinese markets, restaurants or other businesses that catered to the needs and interests of Chinese residents. After the shops closed around 6 p.m., the street became quiet and deserted, aside from the patrons of a few neighborhood bars.

Where we lived was about 8 blocks to Grant Avenue, the heart of Chinatown, This distance from our flat to Chinatown would have been easy to cover as the crow flies. However, this route involved climbing up, and then down, the long steep slopes of Nob Hill or Russian Hill on which Sacramento, Clay, Washington, and Jackson Streets lie. Mother would walk it almost daily to shop for fresh vegetables and Chinese foods. Carrying a shopping bag in each hand, full of fresh vegetables, meat, and other culinary treasures such as char sui bow (barbequed pork buns), she trudged home from Chinatown over the least steep route along Pacific Street in time to prepare dinner.

Chinatown was an adventure for us children, too, as we had never seen Chinese shops, groceries, and restaurants, let alone in such numbers. We explored it with wide-eyed curiosity and these excursions helped us better understand Chinese ways, and, we enjoyed the delicious and relatively inexpensive meals available in Chinese restaurants.

Living Quarters

In comparison to the meager dwelling where we lived in

Macon, the San Francisco residence was luxurious. The flat above the laundromat was vacant shortly before we moved in. Mary's brother-in-law and his friends were hired to paint the entire flat, so that it was sparkling fresh and clean for our arrival. We had no furniture at all, having left all our crate furniture, dilapidated beds, and wobbly chairs behind. Within a short period, we bought all the necessary home furnishings, even a coffee table and a pair of end tables. We were thrilled to have our very first flush toilet inside the living quarters. For the first time in our lives, we had a real bathtub, with a shower. The only 'tub' I had used before was a galvanized iron washtub about two feet in diameter and one foot high, in which I used to wash my dirty feet before going to bed. Our first vacuum cleaner was exciting for someone who had only a broom to sweep floors with. It was thrilling watch it suck up dust balls while the machine roared loudly. In the kitchen, another first for us was our new four-burner gas stove that also had an oven. Mother learned to bake, and made cupcakes as well as cakes.

Perhaps the most exciting new acquisition was our first television set, a 16-inch RCA black and white set enclosed in a real walnut cabinet. We quickly learned to enjoy the popular network programs. As a sports fan, I was excited to be able to watch college football games and major league baseball games. Because television is a visual medium, Mother watched and enjoyed some programs even though she did not fully understand the dialogue. Television introduced Mother to many aspects of American life, fictional though the presentations were. She enjoyed such universally appealing shows such as *I Love Lucy*, for instance, or variety and comedy programming such as the *Show of Shows*. Also, by viewing commercials she became better acquainted with American customs and values.

Although our Polk Street flat had a fireplace in the living room, we never used it because Mother worried that it might be a fire hazard. The dining room had a built-in buffet in for storing dishes and cups. Behind the kitchen, we even had a room with a pantry as well as two wash sinks that I found very handy when I later converted the space to serve as a photography darkroom.

Jean had the front bedroom with its bay windows that looked out on Polk Street. George and I shared the largest bedroom, at the back of the flat, next to the third bedroom that Mother, and later Father, used. An added convenience was separate wash basins in each of the two back bedrooms. The bathroom was split in two, with one room containing a toilet and the other holding a bathtub-shower and a wash basin. Suddenly we had ample plumbing facilities, so rarely did we have to wait to clean up as we often did in Macon. We were now in seventh heaven.

Father Rejoins Us in San Francisco

Four years after the rest of us came to San Francisco, Father sold the laundry to join us and Mother lost her head-of-household role. She must have had mixed feelings about her loss of the authority and autonomy she had had during his absence. They now shared responsibility for operating the laundromat. The workload was considerably lighter for Father than the heavy physical and temporal demands he had in the laundry in Georgia. To a lesser extent, Jean,

George, and I also had to readjust. I was no longer the male head of household. Moreover, since we had not been with Father for almost four years (aside from my one summer with him in 1953 and a brief visit he made to San Francisco in 1955 to look for a second real estate property), he seemed almost a stranger.

Figure 41 Father and Mother at work in our laundromat, c. 1957.

Father relished his move to San Francisco. For one thing, the weather was infinitely more agreeable, and San Francisco, cooled by the typical fog from the Pacific, was never oppressively hot as it was in Georgia during the summer. In fact, even the few days when it was hot in San Francisco, the evening fog of summer would roll in around late afternoon and quickly lower the temperature to levels that were rather chilly.

Finally, Father found social outlets that he never could have had in Macon. He met other Chinese men in community centers. He befriended a Chinese artist who he commissioned a watercolor painting of a famous Chinese legend in which an ancient poet, once a favorite advisor to the Emperor, stands on a mountaintop overlooking a river. According to the legend, the poet jumped into the river and drowned to protest the Emperor's corrupt regime.[73] Father was quite proud and excited to hang the painting on the living room wall.

Figure 42 Father commissioned this painting inspired by ancient martyred poet, Qu Yuan.

We were surprised to learn of Father's sudden interest in ancient Chinese history, an aspect of Father that we never witnessed in Macon. He may have had such interests but he could never develop them while he was working all day.

Father also introduced me to *Tai Chi Chuan*, the ancient slow movement meditative exercise that when performed at a faster pace is

---

[73] The poet was Qu Yuan, a sage who served in the court of Emperor Huai during the Warring States period (475 - 221 BC). His enemies persuaded the Emperor to exile Qu Yuan. In despair over how the country was run, he protested by drowning himself. Legend has it that his distraught followers raced to the river to try to rescue him. This incident is the inspiration for the traditional Chinese festival that features dragon boat races.

related to forms of Asian martial arts. He bought me a book, and encouraged me to learn it for the health benefits it is believed to bestow. He started reading Chinese Taoist treatises such as "Truth and Nature" (*Daw Der Jing*). Having no inkling previously that Father had any philosophical interests, I was impressed and excited to discover this intellectual side of my father.

Because the laundromat was not very profitable, Father and Mother decided to invest in a second apartment building to generate more income. For over a year before Father's move to San Francisco, Mother spent countless hours investigating possible properties, analyzing location, price, loan requirements, and profitability. She chose an 8-unit apartment building in a desirable area at the corner of Presidio and Clay Streets on the very edge of the prestigious area of Presidio Heights. Managing an apartment house provided a good income for full retirement, but it was not always easy, as tenants would often summon Father to repair plumbing, electrical, or heating problems. He learned how to do most of these repairs himself.

Sometime in the early 1960s Mother and Father closed the laundromat and during the ensuing 20 years or so, rented the space to a succession of tenants ranging from a typewriter shop, toy store, and restaurants. At one point, a Chinese tenant opened a hobby shop that featured a slot car racing setup in the store. Very popular with early adolescent boys, it also attracted George who soon was working informally for the owner.

Mother and Father now had more leisure time to enjoy the hard-earned fruits of their labor, and to spend time doting on their grandchildren, Richard, Liz, Marilyn, and Grace. In 1959 Jean married a Chinese exchange student from Singapore, Dennis Oh whom she met at the University of Southern California in Los Angeles. They found employment in the San Francisco area, Dennis as a structural engineer and Jean as an elementary school teacher. Soon, Mother and Father welcomed their fifth grandchild, Derrick in 1963. Later, Jean and Dennis adopted another son, Darryl, who arrived from Korea at the age of 8.

Mother delighted her grandchildren when they visited, particularly when they stayed overnight. She made "grandma burgers" from scratch and cooked them in batches late at night. Then, the next morning she steamed them hot and served her creation for breakfast. She also loved to bake cupcakes, to the delight of her grandchildren, which she also produced in large quantities.

At Thanksgiving and Christmas, Mother hosted the family gathering, preparing a large turkey, dressing, and sweet potatoes. At Christmas she took pleasure in buying gifts for the grandchildren, especially mechanical toys, wind-up or battery-driven animated Santas or stuffed animals. She would also give the grandchildren money in the traditional Chinese red envelopes, *lai see*, not only at Christmas but at Chinese New Years and other special occasions.

Stock Market Trading

In Macon, Father knew nothing about the stock market even though Merrill, Lynch, Pierce, Fenner, and Bean, the big stock brokerage had an office nearby on Third Street near the Dempsey Hotel. But the front window of the firm was completely shielded by closed venetian blinds that prevented any one seeing inside. I was too young to know what a stock brokerage firm did and always wondered if some secret activities were going on.

After retiring and moving to San Francisco, Father learned about stocks, probably from contacts in Chinatown. Before long, he opened an account with a major brokerage firm that employed brokers who spoke fluent Cantonese. Soon I was being summoned by Father to read annual reports and explain them to him. I was not of much help as every company report was glowing with success and to me all of them seemed to be good investments. Father dabbled in trading stocks with mixed success and he made all of the stock investment decisions. Mother never would have been allowed any participation although she was also developing an interest in stock trading. Mother was even less informed than Father about the stock market, but somehow she felt she knew enough to always offer her advice, which invariably included "buy IBM." Somehow she had learned that IBM often split its shares. But she didn't seem to realize that you would still have the same amount of money after a split of stock because the value of each share is reduced in proportion to the number of newly created shares. She seemed to think you that the extra shares be still worth the same amount as it was before it was split.

My Career and Isolation from Chinese Contact

I was a good but not brilliant undergraduate student, who still managed to get admitted to graduate school in 1959 to study psychology at Northwestern University in Evanston, Illinois, just north of Chicago. Father readily accepted my decision to leave the Bay area without much objection, but Mother was not pleased that I would be so far away from the family. They really did not understand what I wanted to study, and I could not explain in Chinese what 'experimental psychology' was.

I had become more 'Chinese' living in the San Francisco area during my high school and college years with the many Chinese students there but over the next decade I would lose much of my Chinese identity because there were relatively few Chinese in areas where I lived. It was almost like being back in Georgia as far as being isolated from other Chinese Americans.

First, I spent three years at Northwestern University, located in a predominantly upper middle class white community just north of Chicago. Although Northwestern provided a strong and supportive environment that allowed me to develop professionally working with outstanding faculty and bright graduate students, this was at the price of ethnic isolation. Affirmative action policies had not yet been implemented and minority students were few[74] in number and weak in power.

During the early 1960s when I was at Northwestern, civil rights activism increased across the nation, yet the social and political climate on this campus was rather conservative. For instance, when a barbershop near the campus refused to cut black students' hair, student protest was minimal. At times when I felt lonely from being "ethnically

[74] I did have the good fortune of sharing a garret apartment with the sole black sociology graduate student, Troy Duster. He seemed to spend more time listening to his vast classical music record collection and playing the cello than he did studying, but he had me fooled as he went on to a distinguished academic career and in 2005 became President of the American Sociological Association.

isolated" in Evanston, I would go to Chicago's Chinatown for a Chinese meal or I would seek out the company of the one other Chinese graduate student in my Department.[75]

My parents were proud, and also relieved when I completed my doctoral studies in 1962, because I then took a teaching appointment in Long Beach, California. Although I was still 400 miles from San Francisco, it was not as bad as my being 2,000 miles away. On the other hand they were beginning to worry about me still being single at age 26. I too started to feel anxious, but because there were few Chinese in the Long Beach area during those years so that the prospect of my meeting, dating, and marrying a Chinese woman was not good. Mother started talking about looking around Chinatown, or even Hong Kong, to match me with an eligible Chinese girl. However, I refused to have anything to do with that solution.

In 1965 after three years teaching in Long Beach, I left California for York University to Toronto where I had received an excellent offer for a faculty position at this new and promising institution. However, during the middle 1960s the population in the area was primarily white so once again I was isolated from contact with other Chinese.

While I was teaching in Toronto, I realized or finally resigned myself to the fact that I lived and worked in a primarily white, non-Chinese society. Consequently, I decided to place less importance on race and ethnicity in my romantic relationships than on character and

---

[75] Aside from both being Chinese, Rod Wong and I were also interested in similar aspects of Psychology and became close lifelong friends.

personal qualities.

It was not that I thought of myself as 'white' as much as I did not obsess about being 'Chinese.'[76] Once in a while I might catch a glimpse of myself in a reflection and suddenly remember, 'Oh, I'm Chinese,' but most of the time I ignored or suppressed awareness of my ethnicity.[77] If I had grown up and lived most of my life in many urban areas of California, things would surely have been different as my identity as Chinese could be reinforced on a daily basis through shared experiences with other Chinese. But given my history of ethnic isolation, I resolved to make the best of things and tried to focus on the best qualities of both the Chinese and white aspects of my upbringing. This resolution,[78] placing less attention on my Chinese identity, expanded the field of eligible mates and enabled me in 1968 at age 31 to marry. Despite my mother's urging to marry a Chinese, my wife of 37 years, Phyllis, is *not* Chinese. Together, we returned to Long

---

[76] When I taught college during the 1960s in either Long Beach or in Toronto, where Chinese were few then, I was less conscious of ethnic identity. But whenever I went to San Francisco to visit family my ethnic awareness resurfaced. Consciousness of my ethnicity depended on the population mix around me. Since for most of my life, there were few Chinese in my surroundings, this aspect of personal identity was not salient. But with the large influx of Asians in California since 1965, ethnic identity has increasingly become an important personal concern.

[77] The reader is correct in thinking that writing and researching for this memoir reflect a renewed value of Chinese identity for me. This change is in part due to the fact that since 1981 I have been fortunate to have directed two federally funded mentoring programs involving over 300 ethnic minority students interested in pursuing Ph.D. degrees in diverse fields. Working closely with these outstanding students has helped me to recognize the dominant role of ethnic identity on many aspects of their lives.

[78] My solution was flawed because ethnicity does not vanish even though one ignores it because many others still focus on it. This can be positive; for example, I did not think of myself as a *Chinese* psychology professor, but many non-Chinese did. By noticing my ethnicity at a time when there were very few Chinese psychology professors, they saw that a Chinese person can teach psychology.

Beach, where I resumed teaching at the university I had left three years before.

Mother and Father had waited so long for me to marry that they accepted Phyllis wholeheartedly despite the fact that she was *not* Chinese. Phyllis was very interested in and knowledgeable about Chinese customs and culture, and enjoyed all manner of Chinese foods, all of which endeared her to them. Similarly, even though I was not Jewish, Phyllis's parents soon accepted me wholeheartedly as their son-in-law.

Figure 43 Phyllis and I with my parents at our 1968 San Francisco reception.

The birth of our son Jeff in 1969 provided one more reason for us to travel more often to visit my parents in San Francisco who doted on their new grandson. Father even made several plane trips to Long Beach to visit us even though he disliked traveling. Of course, we knew it was mainly to see Jeff. Sadly, he died before he could meet our second son, Tomy, who was 18 months old when we adopted him from Korea five years later.

With a large extended family all living fairly close by, this period was probably the happiest time for my parents. They lived in a Chinese community with familiar language, foods, and customs. The weather was invigorating, a vast improvement over the climatic conditions they endured all those years in Macon. They were respected and indulged by their two sons-in-law and daughter-in-law. And, they got to enjoy watching their grandchildren grow up.

Mother Becomes a Citizen

Becoming a citizen, in itself, was not a meaningful or necessary goal for her own needs. Mother was not interested in being able to vote but she may well have had some concerns about being deported even though she had been in the U. S. for about 30 years. For during the Cold War climate of the 1950s, a strenuous renewed effort was started by the federal government to curb 'paper immigration' of Chinese using false identities. The Immigration and Naturalization Service offered a controversial and politicized Chinese Confession Program for Chinese who had entered the country illegally with false papers in exchange for assistance in gaining legal status. Confession would also allow relatives to change their names to reflect their kinship.

Despite such assurances, some Chinese were deported.[79]

Under these circumstances, many immigrants sought U. S. citizenship even if they never intended to exercise its voting privileges. In the late 1950s Mother enrolled in an English language class at a Chinese church and studied late into the wee hours night after night for several years. Mother pored over her English composition books

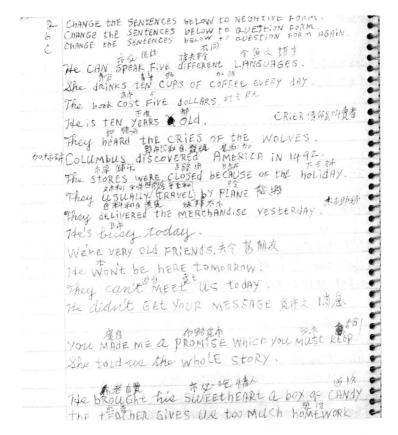

Figure 44 One of Mother's countless, and tedious, English homework drills.

---

[79] The program was also divisive, as confession by one person had a ripple effect on all family members, some who may not have wanted to participate. Mae M. Ngai "Legacies of Exclusion: Illegal Chinese Immigration During the Cold War Years" *Journal of American Ethnic History*, 18 no. 1 (1998): 3-36.

and her Chinese-English dictionary. She filled numerous notebooks with meticulously handwritten exercises on unfamiliar topics that she learned by rote. She had to learn correct grammatical forms, know verb tenses, and avoid double negatives, etc, as the lessons were not limited to history, geography, and civics. Often when I came home well after midnight I would find she had fallen asleep at the table with her head resting on her notebook.

In 1964, finally, Mother passed and became a naturalized citizen of the United States. She was proud of her achievement, as we all were. However, I think she voted only once because she learned that voting makes one eligible for jury duty, an intimidating task because she did not feel her command of English was adequate.

Figure 45 Mother's U. S. Naturalization Certificate, 1964.

Mother and Father's Overdue Visit to Hong Kong

In 1971, Mother and Father finally were able to take a long overdue trip to Hong Kong, the place from where 42 years earlier they had embarked for Gam Saan. This was the first and only 'vacation' they ever had together. Unfortunately, at this time, the Communists did not allow visits to mainland China

Figure 46 Mother and Father relax on their 1971 visit to Hong Kong.

In 1974, following President Nixon's 1972 Beijing visit, the U.S. 'ping pong' diplomacy established better U.S.-China relations. Overseas relatives of Chinese were then allowed to enter the country, and Mother, now widowed, returned alone to her home village after an absence of almost 50 years. She did not worry about taking the long trip by herself. Fearless, she was very excited about her trip, and purchased many presents to take to her family. Concerned, as usual, about health, she carefully boiled several gallons of water, which she lugged in plastic jugs for her journey from San Francisco to China. Mother visited her mother, then in her 90s, and who would eventually lived to a ripe age of 95. It must have truly been an emotional meeting although Mother never disclosed these feelings to us. All she reported was that she and her mother stared at each other for quite a while unable to recognize each other.

Father's Death

Sometime in late 1971, Father suddenly, so it seemed, became noticeably frailer. He had lost weight, and lacked energy. Still, it was a shock to learn that he had developed liver cancer, which by the time the diagnosis was made in early 1973, had advanced. At times, Mother who could be harshly insensitive berated Father for not having taken better care of his health. With a couple of months he died. His death was the first significant one that our family had faced and we were devastated.

It is difficult to know how Mother felt emotionally. She never discussed her feelings about most personal matters with us. Certainly she grieved, but she did not become hysterical or immobilized. In part, because we were ourselves distraught over his death we did not pay as much attention to her reactions as we probably should have.

Still, we may not have understood or interpreted the expression of her feelings correctly because our American ways of showing grief may have differed from Chinese feelings about expressions of public grief. If there was any concern about how well she would be able to manage on her own, those doubts were dispelled in short order. She soon proved that she was amply capable of taking charge of her future.

Thriving as a Widow

Mother tackled the management of the apartment house pretty much on her own. She also began to visit stock brokerage offices and, like Father, opened accounts with financial firms that employed Cantonese-speaking brokers. Soon she became an active stock trader and even appeared in a Chinese newspaper advertisement for a firm seeking Chinese clients. As she developed sufficient knowledge about the mechanics of trading, she dropped her Chinese-speaking brokers in favor of English-speaking ones who worked at discount brokerage firms to save on commissions. Each business day she would either telephone or go down to confer with her broker on her way to or back from Chinatown.

Since Mother knew little about the businesses of various corporations, their economic outlook, or the many factors that influence stock prices, how could she hope to succeed in trading stocks? Sometimes, it seems, ignorance is bliss. Perhaps, too much knowledge can impede decision-making. Limited as she was in her technical knowledge of economics and finance, Mother based her decision-making entirely on trends in price movement, with some success.

Figure 47 Chinese newspaper ad of Mother with her stockbroker.

By simply studying stock ticker tape changes as quotations flashed across the monitor screen in the brokerage offices, she focused on stocks that showed both high volume and generally or rapidly changing price trends. Those were her buy or sell signals! She would spend endless hours keeping meticulous records of her trading transactions and the date and amount of every dividend received.

Once when I examined her brokerage statement, I noticed she had purchased shares of several small, high-flying stocks, including the company that published *Playboy* magazine. When I asked if she knew what this particular company did, she admitted she had no idea, but she had purchased it when she noticed that its stock was moving up. Even though she would have disapproved of their business, I doubt if she would have dumped the stock. Still, I tried to urge her to invest more cautiously, given that she did not know much about financial and business issues, and advised her to buy safer, more conservative stocks.

She replied was that she wanted only volatile stocks. During that era, American Telephone and Telegraph, called "Ma Bell," was the quintessential safe stock for retirees because it paid a good and steady dividend and maintained a stable price. Yet Mother defied this safe strategy recommended for the elderly, and declared outright that she did not want to buy stock in companies like American Telephone which she felt was better suited for young people because its price rose slowly, if at all. It was not the appropriate stock or her, she argued, "I don't have that much time left...I need to buy those stocks that move fast!"

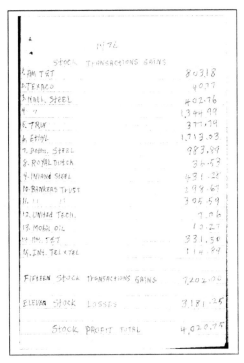

Figure 46   Mother's record of her stock market investing, 1976.

Trading Options

We had been surprised when we learned of her avid interest in stocks and then later totally astonished when we learned that she had begun to trade in options,[80] volatile and speculative financial instruments. Instead of buying or selling the actual stock, the purchaser only pays for the 'option' to buy or sell specific stocks at a certain price within the next few months. When the stock price changes a lot, the holder of the option stands to make bigger profits for a given amount of money because an option costs much less than the stock that it controls. But if the price change of the underlying stock does not change sufficiently to be profitable within its limited life period, the options expire worthless. For someone without much experience and poor English, it is amazing that she was able to do reasonably well trading such complex financial instruments as options.

Long Distance Mothering

As mentioned earlier, in 1962 after I finished my Ph.D. studies in psychology, I began teaching at Long Beach State College, a fairly new and rapidly-expanding state university campus located about 400 miles south of San Francisco, a distance that reduced my direct contact with them to visits during spring or Christmas vacations.

Mother, from her diligent work preparing for her citizenship examination, had acquired considerable proficiency with English.

---

[80] An option is riskier because it has a relatively short life, expiring in anywhere from a few days to a few months. In contrast, with stocks you own you can hold them 'forever' unless the company goes bankrupt. Hence a stock that goes down in value may eventually go back up if you can wait long enough. One incentive for trading options is that you gain a lot of leverage as the cost is a fraction of the same amount of stock. It is like paying a down payment and being able to put a hold on the merchandise.

Occasionally, as a way of practicing her new language skill she wrote letters to me imparting the same motherly advice that she had dispensed as we were growing up.

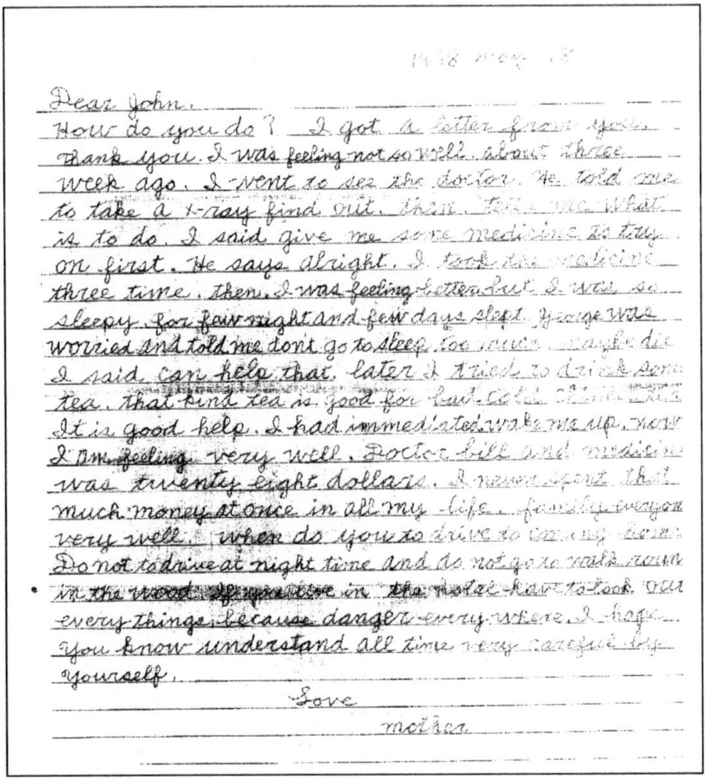

Figure 49 Mother informing me about treatment for a health problem.

Mother usually couched her advice in the context of her own life experiences. In one letter, shown below, after thanking me for contributing toward a new refrigerator, she talks about her frugal life habits, asks me why I thought she was that way, points out how much she had sacrificed to provide for us, ending with the view that she no longer needed to worry since we could now provide for ourselves.

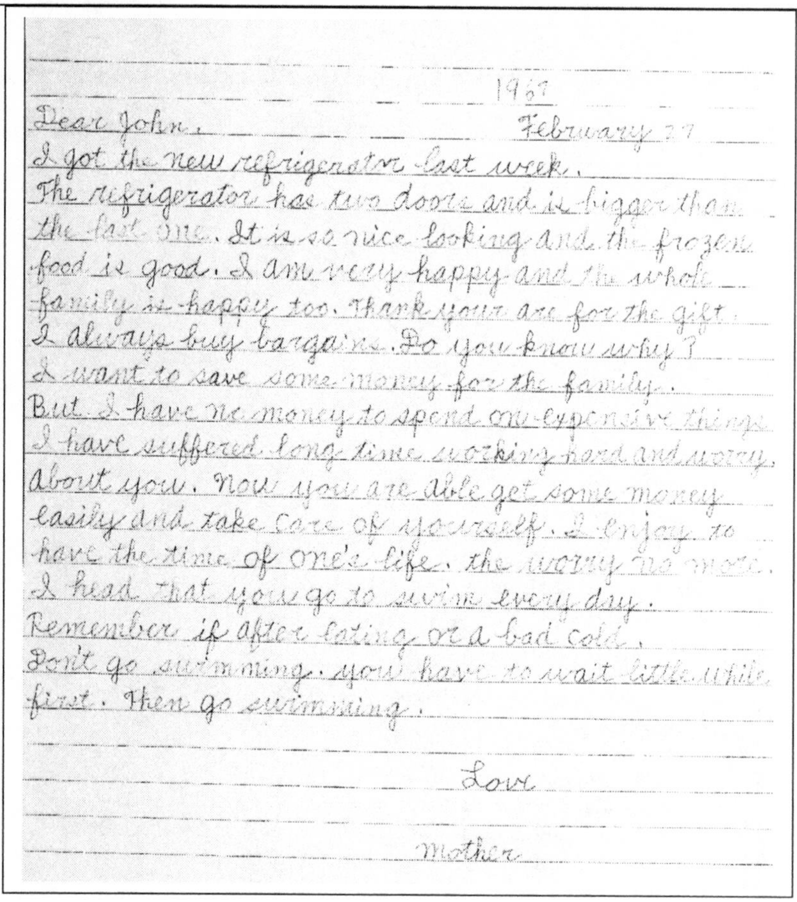

1967

Dear John, February 27

I got the new refrigerator last week.
The refrigerator has two doors and is bigger than
the last one. It is so nice looking and the frozen
food is good. I am very happy and the whole
family is happy too. Thank your are for the gift.
I always buy bargains. Do you know why?
I want to save some money for the family.
But I have no money to spend on expensive things
I have suffered long time working hard and worry
about you. Now you are able get some money
easily and take care of yourself. I enjoy to
have the time of one's life. the worry no more.
I head that you go to swim every day.
Remember if after eating or a bad cold.
Don't go swimming. you have to wait little while
first. Then go swimming.

Love

Mother

Figure 50 Mother's thank you letter plus financial advice.

In another letter, shown below, she advises me to not work too hard, expressing fear that doing so would make me "get crazy." She goes on to hint that perhaps I should get married so she would not have to worry so much about me being alone.

Even though she was many miles away, Mother's guiding voice still managed to exert its influence on my life in the form of these words of caution penned in her best handwriting. The moral is that you can move, but you can never escape from your mother's lessons.

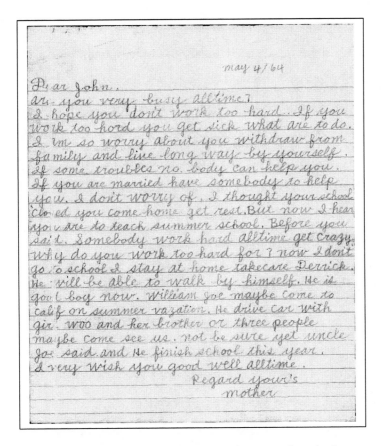

may 4/64

Dear John,

are you very busy alltime?
I hope you don't work too hard. If you
work too hard you get sick what are to do.
I'm so worry about you withdraw from
family and live long way by yourself.
If some troubles no body can help you.
If you are married have somebody to help
you. I don't worry of. I thought your school
closed you come home get rest. But now I hear
you are to teach summer school. Before you
said. Somebody work hard alltime get crazy.
Why do you work too hard for? now I don't
go to school I stay at home takecare Derrick.
He will be able to walk by himself. He is
good boy now. William joe maybe come to
calif on summer vazation. He drive car with
gir woo and her brother or three people
maybe come see us. not be sure yet uncle
joe said and He finish school this year.
I very wish you good well alltime.
                    Regard your's
                         mother

Figure 51 Mother urging me to marry and not to work too hard.

Sponsoring Her Brother and His Family to the U. S.

Mother was excited to have the opportunity to sponsor her brother, Kwan Chong Fan, and his family in China to immigrate to the U. S. The Immigration Act of 1965 broadly liberalized the criteria for entering the United States by eliminating quotas for different countries of origin and she welcomed the chance to help her brother and his family.

Her brother had only been 8 or 9 when Mother left China in 1928, but 50 years later in 1978, she still felt a strong desire to bring his family to the United States for better opportunities. However, by then he was nearing retirement, and reluctant to come. Finally, he consented to apply, for he realized it would be good for his children to have the opportunity to live in the U. S. Mother enlisted the aid of Uncle Joe's oldest son to guarantee employment for Chong Fan in their laundry in Atlanta, even though he was not required to accept that job once he gained entry if he had other opportunities.

The path to gaining the entry of her brother and his family, a wife, two sons and a daughter, was difficult. Filled with delays and red tape, it required almost a decade to complete. The application was made in 1978, but was denied at least twice, in 1982 and in 1985, for missing or incomplete documentation of information. Mother regarded this excessive delay was another instance of prejudice against Chinese. However, she never wavered, and her persistence paid off when in 1986, their entry was finally approved.

Mother's nephews, Jack and Sam, and her niece, Yu Sha, quickly adapted and prospered in the U. S. All of them married and have children, and all live in the San Francisco area. Mother gladly loaned her nephew money to start his own business for a better life for his family in America. For the most part, Mother had minimal subsequent contact with them after they got settled even though they lived a few blocks away. In hindsight, it almost seems that she avoided them, perhaps because she felt they might become dependent on her and expect too much from her. Or, perhaps she wanted them to make their own way without any interference from her. She never discussed the situation with us.

A Surprise "Green Card" Marriage

Mother was always very independent and resilient so adjusting to widowhood was not a great problem for her after Father's death. Mary and Jean still lived near San Francisco and visited her and George often. However, as their own families grew, they had less time to visit. Also, it was physically more difficult to visit as Mary and Ed had moved their family from San Francisco long ago to Foster City, a rapidly growing suburb about 20 miles to the south. Jean and her husband Dennis moved to several nearby locations, which were also inconvenient to San Francisco. And, being 400 miles to the south in Long Beach, I was the least frequent visitor.

As Mother aged, she developed the usual aches and pains- arthritis and skin ailments, for which she sought Chinese folk remedies. An old Chinese herbal doctor's remedies in fact proved very helpful to her and she felt very fortunate to have met him. In time, the 'doctor,' a somewhat inept businessman, ran into financial difficulties and found himself facing eviction from his store. Mother was concerned for him, and since her three-bedroom Polk Street flat had a good deal of space and an extra bedroom, she invited him to store his medicinal brews and herbs there, and to live in one of the bedrooms. He was extended cooking privileges, and prepared his own meals. Mother never said anything specific about these arrangements to us, and none of us felt it was appropriate to demand any explanations from her about her personal life.

The arrangement was apparently a mutually beneficial one: Mother was able in this way to repay the doctor for his remedies and at the same time find companionship. The doctor, of course, benefited as he had no other place to stay. At some point, however, the relationship soured, and arguments began. On one occasion, George witnessed a shouting match turn physical when the doctor shoved Mother, causing her to fall. George reported this ugly incident to Mary. We then realized we had a serious and unacceptable problem on our hands.

Mary exerted pressure on the doctor to move out of the premises, but he sensed he had the upper hand and refused though she offered to help him find another place to live. Finally, she summoned a policeman to ask him to leave, but without any success. The doctor simply ignored the demands and given that no charges were filed, the police could take no action. After all, he had been living there rent-free for some time so he was not willing to leave. Eventually, alarmed and concerned about possible future violence, Mary obtained a restraining order issued by a seniors' advocacy organization and she immediately moved Mother out of the Polk Street flat to her own home for safety.

Shortly after these events, I went to San Francisco for a week during spring vacation. Angry and worried, I tried to determine the best course of action. I decided to spend the night in the flat with George and the doctor. I did not have enough Chinese-speaking ability, and the doctor knew even less English so it was impossible for us to discuss the situation. This was just as well, for there was no telling what I would have said to him if I thought he could understand me. As it turned out, although he was a guest in the flat, for whatever reason, Mother had never provided him with a front door key. Whenever he went out, he was entirely dependent on Mother or George being home to let him back in. Mother was shrewd enough to make sure that she had control over matters that way.

On my second day there, the doctor left to go to Chinatown. That evening when he was ready to come back to the flat, he phoned around 6 to announce that he would arrive back at 7. He wanted to be sure I would be there so he could gain entry. In an instant, my anger rose and, on impulse, I resolved not to let him back in. When he arrived, he repeatedly rang the doorbell but I ignored it and he eventually left. Because it was a cold rainy night, my sense of vengeance was heightened. However, my glee was short-lived and replaced with anxiety because he soon returned, accompanied by two white police officers. When I opened the door, the officers politely asked me what was going on. They informed me that the doctor had claimed that he lived there and that he was being refused entry.

As calmly as I could, I told the officers that what he said was true, but that we currently had a restraining order against him that indicated he could not be within 15 feet of my mother, who also resided there. They examined the restraining order and sided with me much to the doctor's consternation and dismay. The police could plainly see that he had no key to the flat and was outside the premises, while I was on the inside holding a valid legal document prohibiting his presence within 15 feet of Mother. They must have realized he could not maintain this distance if he were allowed back onto the premises. I did not offer information that Mother was no longer actually on the premises and I was not asked where she was. In view of these circumstances, the police upheld my action to deny him entry.

The next morning the doctor returned again with another policeman but this time it was a Chinese officer. I feared the worst since he could now plead his case to someone who spoke his language. The officer politely informed me the doctor only wanted to enter long enough to gather a few personal belongings. This seemed reasonable, and I consented to the request. After about five or ten minutes I heard them speaking loudly and shouting at each other in Chinese in the back bedroom. They were arguing over some issue but since they were speaking Chinese I could not fully understand the problem. When they finally came to the front of the flat, the officer turned to me, as if to plead his case to me, and complained that the doctor was taking too much time gathering his possessions. He finally pressured the doctor to bring two packed suitcases to the head of the staircase. Then, instead of heading down the stairs, the doctor suddenly headed toward the kitchen, explaining that he wanted to get his food. When he heard this additional request, the officer lost his patience and hurled both suitcases down the stairs where one of them burst open when it hit the threshold. Needless to say, I was startled but secretly pleased at this turn of events. The officer turned to me sheepishly and said something like, 'I'm sorry I had to do that.' My reply, intended to reassure him, was something like, 'Don't worry, I really didn't see what just happened.'

That action probably was the turning point, because the doctor must have concluded that his case was hopeless. He gathered his belongings, repacked them, and then quickly left. I breathed many sighs of relief because things were going so well. I had worried that he might assert squatters' rights as a basis for remaining in the flat, a view that would be seen with sympathy in a city like San Francisco. However, the episode with the Chinese policeman seemed to take the fight out of him and he found refuge elsewhere. Over the next several weeks, he returned many times to pick up as many of his belongings as he could carry by hand. As a precaution, we handed them over to him at the front door rather than allowing him to enter the premises to reclaim them.

In the course of dealing with Mother's situation, as we learned more background, we discovered the problem was much more complicated than we could have imagined. After the physical abuse incident, we took Mother to a Chinese-speaking social worker for assistance in explaining Mother's options to her. In the interview, the social worker discovered, much to our disbelief, that Mother had, in fact, secretly married the doctor about five years earlier. Apparently, it was a green-card marriage that was arranged to prevent the doctor's deportation.

Matters could have been much, much worse. When Mother arranged the marriage, she knew the doctor was penniless, but she did not want to give or loan him money, which she wanted to eventually leave for us, and especially, for George's future care. She did not disclose her true financial resources to the doctor for fear that he might feel entitled to some of her funds. In fact, she had told him that he could not count on any financial help, as all of her financial assets had already been transferred to her children, a deliberate deception designed to protect us.

Although we were stunned when we learned about the marriage, we were also relieved to discover that, for reasons we never learned, she had already divorced the doctor two years prior to our ever knowing there had ever been a marriage. Even then he continued to live in the flat, but we never learned whether it was because he would not leave or because she allowed him to stay. We never asked, nor did she ever explain any aspect of the marriage. We respected her privacy and we also felt awkward in probing into her personal life. Some things are better left alone, we thought.

Moving Out of San Francisco

San Francisco is not an ideal place for the elderly. The homeless had increasingly occupied the streets around the downtown area, including Chinatown. Risks of street crime had increased. For some time, we had been wondering if, or when, we should move Mother and George out of the city, closer to Mary and Jean, but kept postponing the inevitable. Traffic and parking problems in San Francisco made it increasingly difficult to visit them. In addition, the commercial space beneath the flat involved endless problems either with its physical condition or with the tenant. It became obvious that we should move Mother and George to a better location and to do that we would have to sell the Polk Street property and find a suitable replacement. Still, would either Mother or George consent to move out of the stimulating city to live in a safer suburban area and have less access to the things they enjoyed?

The episode with the herb doctor brought matters to an immediate head and motivated us to seek prompt solutions. It was time to move so we began a search for a home on the San Francisco peninsula with a sense of urgency. While waiting for a buyer for the property, in 1991 we rented the Polk Street flat to tenants and bought a small bungalow for Mother and George in San Bruno,[81] a small, pleasant working class town about 15 miles south of San Francisco that retained a 1950s atmosphere along its business district.

Moving all of Mother's possessions that accumulated over more than 40 years was a major undertaking. Both Mother and George were 'pack rats' who acquired things but never discarded anything even if it was not needed or useful. Mother collected rubber bands, twisty ties, MacDonald's condiment packets, and paper napkins. She stockpiled all forms of household supplies. To illustrate, we found closets full of 4-packs of toilet paper; she seemed to have cornered the market. It seems that whenever she saw a good sale on toilet paper, she would buy even though she already had at least 6 years worth of toilet paper. We found dozens of unopened packs of toilet paper in a shade of avocado green that was in vogue back in the 1970s and no longer available. She loved to buy dime store jewelry and trinkets. Her umbrella collection was amazing, only surpassed by her stockpile of shopping bags. Stashed in her closet we found a hoard of a large supply of shopping bags that included both department store and

---

[81] By coincidence, although we did not know it when Mother moved there, the National Archives that contain the immigration records of all Chinese who entered the U. S. at San Francisco, including those of my parents, is located only about a mile from where Mother and George lived in San Bruno.

inexpensive fabric tote bags, most never used. With this supply, she easily could have used a different one each day of the year.

Suburban Isolation

San Bruno turned out to be less convenient for Mother and George than living in the heart of the city. To go to San Francisco to shop for Chinese foods was an all-day expedition even though their new home was located only two blocks away from El Camino Avenue, the main artery that runs from San Francisco south through the heart of the Peninsula and offers easy access to bus service to the city. Soon they were making trips several times each week from their new home to San Francisco.

As Mother grew frail, George had to accompany her on these trips because she began to lose strength in one hand and could not carry or grasp heavy objects. She also became somewhat disoriented and confused at times. Once she got off the bus when she recognized a MacDonald's that she was using as a cue but unfortunately, it was the wrong MacDonald's. Soon it was an ordeal for George to accompany her on these shopping trips. They became increasingly reluctant to go to San Francisco, and they felt very isolated in San Bruno.

Throughout this transition period, Mother always placed George's well-being above her own. Periodically we would suggest that George do some of the cooking both to help Mother and to acquire the self-sufficiency he would need after Mother passed on. But Mother would always insist that he would make a mess or did not want to learn and then proceeded to do all the cooking. George was too crafty to complain and continued to depend completely on her.

Kidney Failure and Dialysis

In 1993, approaching her 84th birthday, doctors discovered that Mother had impaired kidney function, a factor that may have contributed to the incessant itching she suffered in her later years. Ever self-reliant, she tried to treat herself, experimenting with a variety of ointments and creams, and the resulting delay in seeking medical advice may well have aggravated her condition. The prognosis was not good. As her kidneys were failing, she had to undergo dialysis several times a week, with each session requiring about two hours. Surely a very unpleasant experience, Mother was stoic and accepted the uncomfortable treatments, grimacing in pain when an inept attendant failed to do the procedure correctly. Eventually, after two years of dialysis, she was switched to a different treatment method that required the insertion of a shunt in her arm.

Before long, the original shunt could not be used for further treatment sessions. Then a new shunt had to be installed in another location in the arm. She had to endure at least three replacement shunts. At one point she almost refused further dialysis treatments, protesting that she would prefer to die rather than face yet another procedure. Other medical complications arose in 1995 when she had a gall bladder operation, in addition to developing gangrene in a toe that could not be saved.

The beginning of the end came in 1996 when Mother fainted on the street one day near her home. Her blood pressure had a severe drop and she lost the strength in her legs and could not walk. Admitted to a nearby nursing home, she received physical therapy as well as dialysis. She never regained the ability to walk, despite therapy and acupuncture treatment. The loss of her independence depressed her, and us. Confined to her bed in a nursing home, she had little to look forward to. She was not interested in watching television, reading, or socializing, meals were bland and unappetizing. Her days were long and tedious, alleviated only by occasional visits from us. Mary and Jean took turns helping her with her meals, with one coming at lunchtime and the other at dinnertime. George dutifully went to the nursing home daily, and came to realize that Mother was not going to return home. He was saddened, but surprised us by rising to the occasion and taking care of himself. On one hand, he was relieved of the considerable responsibility of looking after Mother, but then he was unhappy that her health was in rapid decline. Faced with the reality that Mother would probably not be improving or coming home, George was able to adjust more quickly to living alone than we thought he would.

Unselfish, as always, Mother would often tell her visitors that they should leave and go about their business after they had been visiting for a short while. She did not want to be a burden to them and preferred being left to herself. In January 1997, six months after entering the nursing home at age 87, she died peacefully. Her ordeal of close to four years of declining health was mercifully over.

Months later when we sorted through her documents and mementoes, we found an old 'sweet pea and rose' talcum powder can. We held our breath as we emptied its contents to see if Mother had left one last surprise for us. It proved to contain only talcum powder.

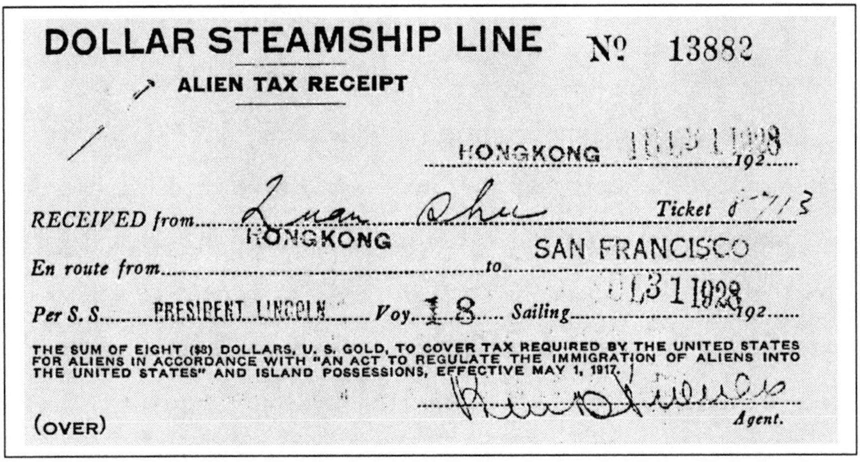

DOLLAR STEAMSHIP LINE № 13882

ALIEN TAX RECEIPT

HONGKONG ... 192...

RECEIVED from ... Ticket 8-713

HONGKONG

En route from ... to ... SAN FRANCISCO

Per S. S. PRESIDENT LINCOLN Voy. 18 Sailing ... 192...

THE SUM OF EIGHT ($8) DOLLARS, U. S. GOLD, TO COVER TAX REQUIRED BY THE UNITED STATES FOR ALIENS IN ACCORDANCE WITH "AN ACT TO REGULATE THE IMMIGRATION OF ALIENS INTO THE UNITED STATES" AND ISLAND POSSESSIONS, EFFECTIVE MAY 1, 1917.

(OVER) ... Agent.

Figure 52 Mother's Alien Tax Receipt when she departed from Hong Kong in 1928

However, carefully preserved with her other papers, we did find her Alien Registration Tax receipt for $8 issued when she left Hong Kong. This document identified the date she departed with Father in 1928 on the S. S. President Lincoln to come to San Francisco. It was the impetus that led me to search for and retrieve her immigration documents from the National Archives, located about a mile from Mother's home in San Bruno. This small slip of paper was the key that opened the door to locating the official records revealing the details of the difficult process my parents faced in gaining entry to this country.

8. Reflections

Although my immigrant parents definitely led difficult lives in Macon, Ga., I ponder what their lives would have been like had they *not* come to the United States. Had they remained in their villages in China, they would have had a hard time as economic and living conditions in the region remained quite poor throughout the twentieth century. Had they survived the economic hardships, they would almost certainly have had to flee to Hong Kong when hostilities with Japan escalated into World War II. Then after the civil war in the late 1940s, they would not have fared well under Mao Zedong's Communist regime. On looking back, my parents' lives in America were not so bad even with language problems, cultural barriers, and racial prejudice. Through hard work and thrift, they managed to earn a living and accumulate a small nest egg that enabled their children to reap many benefits of life and especially education in the United States.

It is also fascinating to look back on what happened to Father in comparison to his two younger brothers. The three brothers' experiences in this country were markedly different. My father, the eldest, had his family with him during his entire time in America. The few years in the 1950s when he remained alone in Georgia made it possible for his wife and children to move to San Francisco, which changed our lives in significant ways as we were no longer the "only Chinese in town."

In contrast, from the late 1930s to the early 1950s Uncle Joe lived alone in Atlanta while his family was in China. His original plan was to earn enough money to send for them, but when the war with Japan broke out, he and his family were separated for many years. Only in 1949 was he able to return to China for a year-long visit and eventually fulfill his plans to bring his wife, and by then four sons, to Atlanta. The two youngest, Henry and William came in 1951 with their mother, James a few years later, and finally the oldest, Hoi Lam and his family in 1963. Uncle Joe and his family decided to stay in Atlanta. I recall that at the time I had hoped they would join us and was disappointed and surprised that they decided to stay in Georgia.

The third brother, Hok Su Lo, did not succeed when he tried to enter the U. S. as a "paper son" in 1936. More than thirty years later, in the early 1970s, his two youngest children, Veronica and Dominic came to the United States to attend college. After graduation, they remained in the U. S., and settled in Knoxville, Tennessee. Both married spouses of Asian descent and remained in the South to work and raise their families in a region with few other Asians. Ironically, Hok Su Lo was finally admitted in about 1990 into the U. S. sponsored by his adult children. Although eager to be near his children and to help care for his grandchildren, arriving in another country at such a late age, he was unable to adjust. Soon his vision failing, he decided to return to China to be near his two older children.

Which brother and family were more fortunate? During the 1950s I thought my parents made a wiser decision in moving to San Francisco than my Uncle Joe who kept his family in Georgia, a highly segregated region, with few Chinese. For our family, the move was appropriate. My father was nearing retirement and my two sisters were approaching the age for marriage. Uncle Joe's oldest son was already married and had his own family and the three younger sons were still not yet of marriageable age so there was no rush to move them to a region to seek prospective Chinese brides.[82] Father's youngest brother had no choice at all since he never did enter the United States to earn a living.

In 1952 I moved from Macon to San Francisco. Since then I have lived in other places across the country. In the past I rarely reflected on my growing up in Georgia, but in recent years I visited Atlanta and Macon to see relatives and friends. These travels let me notice some intriguing contrasts to my memories of the way things were back when I lived in Georgia. For one thing, I see huge improvements in race relations and attitudes toward black people. For another, instead of a handful of Chinese in Atlanta, there has been a substantial increase in the size of Chinese and other Asian populations due to the 1965 immigration law that was fairer to Asians, migration, and births. Nonetheless, I sensed that Chinese in Atlanta are still somewhat isolated from other ethnic and racial groups although perhaps voluntarily rather than from restrictions imposed by societal barriers. Almost all my cousins have married Chinese or other Asians and all but one of my Southern cousins remained in the region. Interestingly, as the next generation reaches adulthood, some are "marrying out" and relocating from the South to places with large Chinese communities like New York, Illinois, and California.

---

[82] Even though they stayed in Atlanta, all of Uncle Joe's sons married Chinese women whereas I, who my parents moved to San Francisco so I could meet Chinese girls ended up marrying a non-Chinese. Even the best of plans do not always work out the way they were intended.

Now I wonder about the importance as well as the ease of achieving and maintaining a distinctive Chinese identity in the South, as opposed to in other regions with large and long-established Chinese communities. Clear answers are elusive. I can only conclude that the lives of Chinese Americans in the South have improved immensely because of improved race relations, liberalized immigration policies, and better China-U.S. relations, and are likely to continue to improve.

Reflections on Our Move

The single most important 'event' in the life of our whole family was the move, in stages, from Macon to San Francisco. No simple undertaking, it required commitment, cooperation, planning, and luck. The idea of moving stemmed from Mother's concern about our future in Macon, where we children lacked opportunities to meet Chinese to marry. She brought up the plan before Mary finished high school. Still, it required Father's absolute commitment to remain alone in Macon four more years to supply us with a source of income. It was difficult to know Father's emotional feelings about making this sacrifice, as he never talked to us about his inner concerns and emotions. He saw it as necessary because he thought we would be better off in California. That was a sufficient basis for his decision.

Father always seemed calm and imperturbable, no matter how trying the circumstances. I rarely saw him lose his temper or get upset. When in 1956 he finally left Macon to move to San Francisco, a journalist wrote a farewell tribute in the local newspaper in which he described Father as "serene." The journalist really captured a key aspect of his personality. This characteristic undoubtedly served him well in dealing with the plight of being an isolated foreigner living in a region and era of strong racial prejudices. He knew he had to be calm to survive and this realization surfaced in several portions of the interview where several intriguing errors occurred. In the excerpt below, the columnist either assumed from the Chinese stereotype that my parents were Confucian, or else my father politely acquiesced when asked if he and Mother were. However, my parents were not 'devout followers' of Confucius, or of any other belief or faith.

> It was touching to interview Mr. Jung just before he left. He is a serene, smiling man of 56. He said that since his was the only Chinese family here, they had led a lonely life with none of the social activities so important to most of us. But the loneliness was overshadowed by the love and affection bestowed upon each member of the family. Occasionally, the late Rev. W. B. Burke, who spent 56 years as a missionary in China, would take the little Jungs to Sunday school. Mr. and Mrs. Jung are devout followers of Confucius.

Figure 53 Excerpt from Walter Bragg, "Not a Chinese in our town for first time in a century." *Macon News,* March 6, 1956, 4.

In other parts of the interview, Father must have answered deceptively, just as he had back in 1921 and 1928 during his immigration interrogation at Angel Island. In the following excerpt, he described how his father came to the U. S. but in fact, his real father never came. However, to be consistent with his "paper son" identity, Father's story about coming to America had to acknowledge his "paper father" being here before his arrival. Then too, his marriage was not to his childhood sweetheart but was an arranged match to a girl whom he had never met. Father twisted the truth because he knew that the concocted romantic tale would be more agreeable to Americans than the true account. He had the presence of mind, after more than 30 years since arriving here, to calmly give the 'right answers.'

> He came here back in 1926 after spending a few years in San Francisco and after looking over business prospects in Augusta, Ga., and Chattanooga, Tenn. He was born in Canton, China, and stayed with his mother while his father came to America to seek his fortune. The mother died before the father could send for them and Frank Jung was 19 years old before enough money could be saved to pay his passage to what he calls "this wonderful country."
>
> ❋ ❋ ❋
>
> AT FIRST, Jung worked for a Chinese operator of a laundry located on Cotton Avenue, where the Barnes building now stands. He worked hard, saved his money and bought out the Chinaman who was then operating the Sam Lee Laundry. Jung established living quarters upstairs and worked 14 to 16 hours a day with one thought in mind . . . to save enough money to go back to Canton and marry his childhood sweetheart and bring her back to Macon. It took him nearly five long years to save up enough but in 1930 he went back to China, married her and brought his bride to Macon.

Figure 54 Another excerpt from Walter Bragg, "Not a Chinese in our town for first time in a century." *Macon News*, March 6, 1956, 4.

I think it was his imperturbability that enabled Father to endure four years alone in Macon after the rest of us left. He did not allow his situation to bother him because he realized that he had to stay behind for us to benefit from being in San Francisco. Mother, too, always presented to outsiders a peaceful and tranquil exterior demeanor. But, difficult and trying situations often upset her. She expressed these negative feelings only to her family. Given her demanding new role in San Francisco, it is surprising how well she managed. Overnight she became the head of our household, with three adolescent children to manage, one of whom was developmentally disabled. While learning to operate a laundromat, she cooked all of our meals. Mother met all of these demands despite her emotionality because she was courageous, resilient, and determined. Not easily discouraged, she did not dwell on the difficulty of her life but set out to get the job done. She was an amazing Grace!

In their own ways, both Mother and Father acted unselfishly, placing the well-being of their children above their own personal needs. They set the example of sacrifice, loyalty, and persistence. They fulfilled their obligations, neither complaining nor bragging. I see them as realists, who knew that life is often difficult, especially for immigrants, and that survival depended on presence of mind, heart, and discipline. My parents were strong enough to adapt to an entirely different way of life in the South, raise a family, and then, decisively move across the entire country to a place they felt provided a better future for their children and themselves.

Lessons from the Chinese Laundry

As the washers and ironers of America's dirty laundry starting about 1850 to beyond 1950, Chinese immigrants served a vital function in their communities. Laundrymen were viewed as servants, paid to do unpleasant tasks no one else wanted to do. Laundrymen, like garbage collectors, received little or no respect. Americans eventually associated

Chinese with laundry to such an extent that the two words became virtually synonymous. Because they worked primarily in this low social status domestic type of work, in other endeavors Americans did not expect high achievements from Chinese. Second-generation Chinese were often embarrassed in public school because they compared their own parents with those of their white classmates who were merchants, skilled craftsmen, or professionals. But, recognizing that laundry work was truly lowly and physically arduous, their children were motivated to rise above their parents who, in turn, wanted their children to obtain better-paying, skilled jobs, be independent business owners, or enter professional careers.

The "Chinese laundry" has virtually vanished, made obsolete in today's world, and the term has been usurped by commercial interests and used as a brand name. I believe, however, it deserves more respect for the indispensable role it played in Chinese immigrant history. Here, as in many other countries, it provided the economic lifeline and fostered the discipline that enabled the laundrymen's children to survive and prosper.

Chronology

1901 Lo Kwok Fui born
1909 Quan Wai Choi born
1921 Lo Kwok Fui emigrates to U. S. to work in laundries
1927 Lo Kwok Fui returns to Taishan for an arranged marriage
1928 Quan Shee and Lo Kwok Fui emigrate to Georgia
1931 Mary born
1934 Eugenia born
1937 John born
1938 George born
1948 Father becomes naturalized citizen
1949 Mother brings Mary to San Francisco
1952 Mother brings Jean, John, and George to San Francisco
1953 Mother operates laundromat in San Francisco
1956 Father sells laundry, moves from Georgia to San Francisco
1964 Mother becomes naturalized citizen
1971 Mother and Father visit Hong Kong
1973 Father dies
1976 Mother and her mother are reunited in Canton
1986 Mother sponsors her brother and family to come to U. S.
1986 Mother enters green card marriage with herbalist
1989 Mother divorces herbalist
1991 Mother and George move from San Francisco to San Bruno
1993 Mother develops kidney failure and requires dialysis
1996 Mother unable to walk and enters nursing home
1997 Mother dies

About The Author

Earning a Ph.D. from Northwestern University in 1962, I taught psychology at California State University, Long Beach for over 40 years and published eight textbooks including *Psychology of Alcohol and Other Drugs*, Sage Publications, 2001.

CPSIA information can be obtained at www.ICGtesting.com
Printed in the USA
LVOW13s1335131113

361159LV00002B/99/P